Susan Sontag

Susan Sontag

◼

The Complete
Rolling Stone
Interview

◼

JONATHAN COTT

Yale
UNIVERSITY PRESS

NEW HAVEN AND LONDON

Published with assistance from the foundation established in memory of Philip Hamilton McMillan of the Class of 1894, Yale College.

Yale University Press books may be purchased in quantity for educational, business, or promotional use. For information, please e-mail sales.press@yale.edu (U.S. office) or sales@yaleup.co.uk (U.K. office).

Designed by Sonia Shannon.
Set in Electra type by Integrated Publishing Solutions.
Printed in the United States of America.

Library of Congress Cataloging-in-Publication Data

Sontag, Susan, 1933–2004.
Susan Sontag : the complete Rolling Stone interview / Jonathan Cott.
    pages   cm
Includes index.
ISBN 978-0-300-18979-7 (cloth : alk. paper)   1. Sontag, Susan, 1933–2004—Interviews.   2. Authors, American—20th century—Interviews.   3. Motion picture producers and directors—United States—Interviews.   I. Cott, Jonathan.   II. Title.
PS3569.O6547Z46 2013
818'.54—dc23
[B]
2013003894

A catalogue record for this book is available from the British Library.

This paper meets the requirements of ANSI/NISO Z39.48-1992 (Permanence of Paper).

10 9 8 7 6 5 4 3 2 1

He becomes a disturber of the intellectual peace, but only at the cost of becoming an intellectual wayfaring man, a wanderer in the intellectual No Man's Land, seeking another place to rest, farther along the road, somewhere over the horizon. They are neither a complaisant nor a contented lot, these aliens of the uneasy feet.

—THORSTEIN VEBLEN

When a person dies, we lose a library.

—OLD KIKUYU SAYING

Contents

■

Preface

■

"THE ONLY POSSIBLE metaphor one may conceive of for the life of the mind," wrote the political scientist Hannah Arendt, "is the sensation of being alive. Without the breath of life, the human body is a corpse; without thinking, the human mind is dead." Susan Sontag agreed. In the second volume of her journals and notebooks (*As Consciousness Is Harnessed to Flesh*), she declared: "Being intelligent isn't, for me, like doing something 'better.' It's the only way I exist. . . . I know I'm afraid of passivity (and dependence). Using my mind, something makes me feel active (autonomous). That's good."

Essayist, novelist, playwright, filmmaker, and political activist, Sontag, who was born in 1933 and died in 2004, was an exemplary witness to the fact that living a thinking life and thinking about the life one was living could be complementary and life-enhancing activities. Ever since the 1966 publication of *Against Interpretation*—her first collection of essays that ranged joyously and unpatroniz-ingly from the Supremes to Simone Weil, and from films like *The Incredible Shrinking Man* to *Muriel*—Sontag never wavered in her loyalties to both "popular" and "high" culture. As she remarked in the preface to the thirtieth-anniversary republication of her book, "If I had to choose between the Doors and Dostoyevsky, then—of course—I'd choose Dostoyevsky. But do I have to choose?"

A proponent of an "erotics of art," she shared with the French writer Roland Barthes not only what he called "the pleasure of the text" but also what she described as his "vision of the life of the mind as a life of desire, of full intelligence and pleasure." In this regard, she was following in the footsteps of William Wordsworth, who, in his "Preface to *Lyrical Ballads*," defined the poet's role as that of "giving immediate pleasure to a human Being"—an undertaking that he took to be "an acknowledgement of the beauty of the universe" and "an homage paid to the native and naked dignity of man"—and insisted that turning that principle into reality was "a task light and easy to him who looks at the world in the spirit of love."

"What makes me feel strong?" Sontag asked herself in one of her journal entries, giving as her answer: "Being in love and work," and affirming her fealty to "the hot exaltations of the mind." Clearly, for Sontag, loving, desiring, and thinking were, at their root, essentially coterminous activities. In her fascinating book *Eros the Bittersweet*, the poet and classicist Anne Carson—a writer whom Sontag greatly admired—proposed that "there would seem to be some resemblance between the way Eros acts in the mind of a lover and the way knowing acts in the mind of a thinker," and Carson added: "When the mind reaches out to know, the space of desire opens"—a sentiment echoed by Sontag in her essay on Roland Barthes when she remarked that "writing is an embrace, a being embraced; every idea is an idea reaching out."

In a 1987 symposium sponsored by PEN American Center that was devoted to the work of Henry James, Sontag expanded on Anne Carson's notion of the indissoluble connection between desiring and knowing. Rejecting the criticisms often made about James's arid and abstract vocabulary, Sontag countered: "His vocabulary is in fact one of munificence, of plenitude, of desire, of jubilation, of ecstasy. In James's world, there is always more—more text, more consciousness, more space, more complexity in space, more food for consciousness to gnaw on. He installs a principle of desire in the novel, which seems to me new. It is epistemological desire, the desire to know, which is like carnal desire, and often mimics or doubles carnal desire." In her journals, Sontag describes the "life of the mind" with the following words: "avidity, appetite, craving, longing, yearning, insatiability, rapture, inclination"; and it is not difficult to imagine that Sontag might have felt that Anne Carson was in fact speaking for both of them when she confessed that "falling in love and coming to know make me feel genuinely alive."

In all of her endeavors, Sontag attempted to challenge and upend stereotypical categories such as male/female and young/old that induced people to live constrained and risk-averse lives; and she continually examined and tested out her notion that supposed polarities such as thinking and feeling, form and content, ethics and aesthetics, and consciousness and sensuousness could in fact simply be looked at as aspects of each other—much like the pile on the velvet that, upon reversing one's touch, provides two textures and two ways of feeling, two shades and two ways of perceiving.

In her 1965 essay "On Style," for example, Sontag wrote: "To call Leni Riefenstahl's *Triumph of the Will* and *Olympiad* masterpieces is not to gloss over Nazi propaganda with aesthetic lenience. The Nazi propaganda is there. But something else is there too . . . the complex movements of intelligence and grace and sensuousness." A decade later, in her essay "Fascinating Fascism," she reversed the pile, commenting that *Triumph of the Will* was "the most purely propagandistic film ever made, whose very conception negates the possibility of the filmmaker's having an aesthetic or visual conception independent of propaganda." Where she once focused on the "formal implications of content," Sontag would explain, she later wished to investigate "the content implicit in certain ideas of form."

Describing herself as both a "besotted aesthete" and an "obsessed moralist," Sontag might well have concurred with

Wordsworth's notion that "we have no sympathy but what is propagated by pleasure" and that "wherever we sympathize with pain it will be found that the sympathy is produced and carried on by subtle combinations with pleasure." So it is not surprising that while Sontag fully embraced the pleasures of what she called "a pluralistic, polymorphous culture," she never ceased from "regarding the pain of others"—the title she gave to the last book she wrote before her death—nor from attempting to ameliorate it.

In 1968 she traveled to Hanoi at the invitation of the North Vietnamese government as part of a delegation of American antiwar activists, an experience that, as she wrote in her journals, "made me re-appraise my identity, the forms of my consciousness, the psychic forms of my culture, the meaning of 'sincerity,' language, moral decision, psychological expressiveness." Two decades later, in the early 1990s, she visited the battered city of Sarajevo on nine separate occasions, bearing witness to the sufferings of its 380,000 residents who were then living under constant siege. On her second visit, in July 1993, she met a Sarajevo-born theater producer who invited her to direct a production of Samuel Beckett's *Waiting for Godot* with some of the city's most accomplished professional actors; and the sounds of sniper fire and the blasts of mortar shells provided a backdrop to both the rehearsals and the performances that were attended by government officials, surgeons from the city's main hospital, and soldiers from the front, as well as many disabled and grieving Sarajevans. "Someone who is perennially surprised that depravity exists," she wrote in *Regarding the Pain of Others*, "who continues to feel disillusioned (even incredulous) when confronted with evidence of what humans are capable of inflicting in the way of gruesome, hands-on cruelties upon other humans, has not reached moral or psychological adulthood." And as she once declared, "There is no possibility of true culture without altruism."

I first met Susan Sontag in the early 1960s when she was teaching, and I was studying, at Columbia University. For three years, I was both a contributor to and one of the editors of the literary supplement to the *Columbia Spectator* — Columbia College's daily newspaper — for which, in 1961, she had written an essay about Norman O. Brown's *Life Against Death* that she would later include in *Against Interpretation*. After reading that essay, I brazenly decided to stop by her office one afternoon to tell her how much I had admired it; and after that first meeting, we met up for coffee on several occasions.

After graduating from Columbia College in 1964, I moved to Berkeley to study English literature at the University of California and immediately found myself in the midst of a great new American social, cultural, and political awakening. "Bliss was it in that dawn to be alive," William Wordsworth had written two centuries earlier at the outset of the French Revolution. Now, once again, people were experiencing a true dramatization of life, and no matter where you went, it seemed as if "there was music in the cafés at night and revolution in the air," as Bob Dylan sang in "Tangled Up in Blue." Reflecting on those days some thirty years later in her preface to the republication of *Against Interpretation*, Sontag wrote: "How marvelous it all does seem, in retrospect. How one wishes some of its boldness, its optimism, its disdain for commerce had survived. The two poles of distinctively modern sentiment are nostalgia and utopia. Perhaps the most interesting characteristic of the time now labeled the sixties was that there was so little nostalgia. In that sense, it was indeed a utopian moment."

One afternoon in 1966 I serendipitously ran into Susan on the Berkeley campus. She informed me that she had been invited by the university to give a lecture, and I told her that I had just started producing and hosting a free-form, late-night radio program for KPFA; mentioned that I and my friend Tom Luddy—who was soon to become the curator for the Pacific Film Archive—were going to be interviewing the filmmaker Kenneth Anger about his movie *Scorpio Rising* later that night; and asked whether she might like to come by to join the conversation, which she did. (In her journals, Susan would include Anger's *Inauguration of the Pleasure Dome* in her list of "Best Films.")

In 1967 I moved to London to become *Rolling Stone* magazine's first European editor, and I continued to work and write for the magazine when I returned to New York City in 1970. Susan and I had a number of friends in common; and over the next several years, both in New York and Europe, we would occasionally find ourselves together at the same dinner parties, film screenings, concerts (both rock and classical), and human rights events. I had always wanted to interview Susan for *Rolling Stone* but had felt reticent about broaching the subject with her. In February 1978, however, I thought that it might be the right time. Her acclaimed book *On Photography* had been published the previous year, and two of her other books were about to appear: *I, etcetera*—a collection of eight short stories that she once described as "a series of adventures with the first person"—and *Illness as Metaphor*. Susan had undergone surgery and treatment for breast cancer between 1974 and 1977, and her experiences as a cancer patient had been the catalyst for her writing that book. So when I finally decided to ask her whether she might consider doing an interview, and suggested that we use those three books as a starting point for our conversation, she unhesitatingly agreed.

There are some writers who feel that taking part in an interview is an experience not unlike that of—as the poet Kenneth Rexroth once remarked after attending a particularly noxious cocktail party—"sticking one's tongue on the third rail before dinner." Italo Calvino was one such person. In his short text "Thoughts Before an Interview," he complained: "Every morning I tell myself: today has to be productive, and then something happens that prevents me from writing. Today . . . what is there that I have to do today? Oh yes, they are supposed to come interview me. . . . *God help me!*" More resistant by far, however, was the Nobel Prize laureate J. M. Coetzee, who, in the middle of an interview with David Attwell, announced: "If I had any foresight, I would have nothing to do with journalists from the start. An interview is nine times out of ten an exchange with a complete stranger, yet a stranger permitted by the conventions of the genre to cross the boundaries of what is proper in conversation between strangers. . . . To me, on the other hand, truth is related to silence, to reflection, to the practice of *writing*. Speech is not a fount of truth but a pale and provisional version of writing. And the rapier of surprise wielded by the magistrate or the interviewer is not an instrument of the truth but, on the contrary, a weapon, a sign of the inherently confrontational nature of the transaction."

Susan Sontag saw things differently. "I like the interview form," she once told me, "and I like it because I like conversation, I like dialogue, and I know that a lot of my thinking is the product of conversation. In a way, the hardest thing about writing is that you're alone and have to set up a conversation with yourself, which is a fundamentally unnatural activity. I like talking to people—it's what makes me not a recluse—and conversation gives me a chance to know what I think. I don't want to know about the audience because it's an abstraction, but I certainly want to know what any *individual* thinks, and that requires a face-to-face meeting."

In one of her journal entries from 1965, Susan avowed: "To give no interviews until I can sound as clear + authoritative + direct as Lillian Hellman in *Paris Review*." Thirteen years later, on a sunny afternoon in mid-June, I arrived at Susan's Paris apartment in the 16th Arrondissement. She and I sat down on two couches in the living room, I placed my cassette tape recorder on the table between them; and as I listened to her clear, authoritative, and direct responses to my questions, it was obvious that she had attained the conversational goal that she had set for herself many years before.

Unlike almost any other person whom I've ever interviewed—the pianist Glenn Gould is the one other exception—Susan spoke not in sentences but in measured and expansive paragraphs. And what seemed most striking to me was the exactitude and "moral and linguistic fine-tuning"— as she once described Henry James's writing style—with which she framed and elaborated her thoughts, precisely calibrating her intended meanings with parenthetical remarks and qualifying words ("sometimes," "occasionally," "usually," "for the most part," "in almost all cases"), the munificence and fluency of her conversation manifesting what the French refer to as an *ivresse du discours*—an inebriation with the spoken word. "I am hooked on talk as a creative dialogue," she once remarked in her journals, and added: "For me, it's the principal medium of my salvation."

But after talking for three hours, Susan told me that she needed to get some rest before going out that night for dinner. I knew that I had already recorded enough material for my *Rolling Stone* interview. To my surprise, however, she informed me that she would soon be moving back to her apartment in New York City for six months; and that since there were still a number of other subjects that she wanted to talk to me about, she asked if I wouldn't mind if we continued and completed our conversation back in New York.

Five months later, on a chilly afternoon in November, I arrived at the spacious penthouse apartment overlooking the Hudson River on Riverside Drive and 106th Street where she lived, surrounded by her library of eight thousand books that she referred to as "my own retrieval system" and "my archive of longing." And in that consecrated spot, she and I sat and talked until late in the evening.

In October 1979, *Rolling Stone* magazine published one-third of my interview with Susan Sontag. Now, for the first time, I am able to present in its entirety the conversation that I was privileged to engage in thirty-five years ago, both in Paris and New York, with the remarkable and inspiring person whose intellectual credo—as I have always thought of it—seems to me to have been most movingly expressed in a short text that she wrote in 1996 entitled "A Letter to Borges":

> You said that we owe literature almost everything we are and what we have been. If books disappear, history will disappear, and human beings will also disappear. I am sure you are right. Books are not only the arbitrary sum of our dreams, and our memory. They also give us the model of self-transcendence. Some people think of reading only as a kind of escape: an escape from the "real" everyday world to an imaginary world, the world of books. Books are much more. They are a way of being fully human.

Susan Sontag

The Complete *Rolling Stone* Interview with Susan Sontag

When you found out that you had cancer four years ago, you immediately started thinking about your illness. I'm reminded of something Nietzsche once wrote: "For a psychologist, there are few questions that are as attractive as that concerning the relation of health and philosophy, and if he should himself become ill, he will bring all of his scientific curiosity into his illness." Is this the way you began to think about Illness as Metaphor?

Well, it's certainly true that the fact that I got sick made me think about sickness. Everything that happens to me is something I think about. Thinking is one of the things I do. If I'd been in an airplane crash and been the only survivor, I might very well have gotten interested in the history of aviation. I'm sure that this experience of the past two and a half years will turn up in my fiction, though very transposed. But as far as that side of me that writes essays, what occurred to me to ask was not, What am I experiencing? but rather, What really goes on in the world of the sick? What are the ideas that people have? I was examining my own ideas because I myself had a lot of the fantasies about illness, and about cancer in particular. I'd never given the question of illness any serious consideration. So if you don't think about things, you're likely to be the vehicle of the going clichés, even of the more enlightened ones.

It isn't as if I'd set myself a task—"Well, now that I'm sick I'm going to think about it"—I just *was* thinking about it. You're lying in the hospital bed and the doctor comes in and they have this kind of *talk* . . . and you listen to it and you start to think about what they're saying to you and what it means and what kind of information you're getting and how you should evaluate it. But then you also think, How *strange* that people talk like this, and you realize that they do so because of the whole set of beliefs that exist in the world of the ill. So you could say that I was "philosophizing" about this—though I don't like to use such a pretentious word because I have too much admiration for philosophy. But to use it in a more general sense, one can philosophize about *anything*. I mean, if you fall in love, you start to think about what love is, if in fact you have the temperament to reflect about it.

A friend of mine, who's a Proust specialist, discovered that his wife was having an affair. He was horribly jealous and wounded, and he told me that he then began to read Proust on jealousy in quite another spirit and began to think about the nature of jealousy and to push those ideas further. And in doing so, he developed a whole other relationship to the texts of Proust and to his own experience. He was really suffering—there was nothing inauthentic about his suffering, and there was certainly no flight from his experience in the fact that he began to think about jealousy in the way that he did—but up to that point he'd never experienced profound sexual jealousy. When he'd previously read about it in Proust, he'd done so in the way one reads anything that's not part of your experience—you don't really connect to it until it is.

I'm not sure that if I were feeling morbidly jealous I'd want to be reading about jealousy at that point. And, similarly, it would seem to me that the fact of being ill and thinking about it in the way you've done must have somehow required an enormous effort and perhaps even necessitated a great deal of detachment on your part.

On the contrary, it would have been an enormous effort for me to *not* think about it. The easiest thing in the world is to think about what's happening to you. Here you are in a hospital thinking you're going to die, and it would have required an enormous effort of detachment for me to *not* think about it. The really enormous effort of detachment was to get out of the period when I was so ill that I couldn't work at all and go back to finish my photography book [*On*

Photography]. That drove me wild. When I finally *could* work, which was about six or seven months after the cancer was diagnosed, I hadn't yet finished the photography essays, even though that book was already done in my head and all the effort left was to execute it and write it out properly and carefully and in an attractive and vivid way—but it drove me crazy to be writing about something I wasn't connected to at that moment. I only wanted to write *Illness as Metaphor*, because all of the ideas for that book came to me very quickly in the first month or two after I got ill, and I really had to force myself to turn my attention to the photography book.

Look, what I want is to be fully present in my life—to be really where you are, contemporary with yourself *in* your life, giving full attention to the world, which *includes* you. You are not the world, the world is not identical to you, but you're in it and paying attention to it. That's what a writer does—a writer pays attention to the world. Because I'm very against this solipsistic notion that you find it all in your head. You don't, there really is a world that's there whether you're in it or not. And if you have a tremendous experience, to me it's much easier to connect your writing to what is actually happening to you rather than to try to retreat from it by becoming involved in something else, because then you're just splitting yourself into two parts. People said I must have been detached to write *Illness as Metaphor*, but I wasn't detached at all.

Might "distant" be a more accurate word? I've noticed that it's a word that comes up quite often in your writings in different contexts, such as when you remark in your essay "On Style" that "all works of art are founded on a certain distance from the lived reality which is represented. . . . It is the degree and manipulating of this distance, the conventions of distance, which constitute the style of the work."

No, not distant. Maybe you know more about what I did than I do . . . and I'm not being ironic, because it's very possible I don't fully understand this process. But I didn't feel distant at all. Writing is not usually enjoyable for me. It's often very tiresome and tedious because I go through so many drafts when I write. And despite the fact that I had to wait a year to begin work on *Illness as Metaphor*, it was one of the few things that I wrote fairly quickly and with pleasure because I could connect with all the things that were happening every day in my life.

For about a year and a half I was going to the hospital three times a week, I was hearing this language, I was seeing the people who are victims of these stupid ideas. *Illness as Metaphor* and the essay I wrote about the Vietnam War are perhaps the only two instances in my life when I knew that what I was writing was not only true but actually useful and helpful to people in a very immediate, practical way. I don't know if my book on photography is useful to anybody except in the most general sense that it adds to people's consciousness and makes things more complicated, which I think is always good. But I know people who have sought proper medical treatment because of reading *Illness as Metaphor*—people who weren't getting anything other than some kind of psychiatric treatment and who are now getting chemotherapy because of it. That's not the only reason I wrote it—I wrote it because I feel that what I said was true—but it's a great pleasure to write something that can be useful to people.

Following Nietzsche's idea that "in some it is their deprivations that philosophize, in others their riches and strengths," it seems interesting that while suffering from your illness, your "deprivations" didn't result in a philosophically "ill" work. In fact you produced something very rich and strong.

I thought that when this started ... well, of course, I was told it was likely that I'd be dead very soon, so I was facing not only an illness and painful operations, but also what I thought might be death in the next year or two. And besides feeling the dread and the terror, as well as the physical pain, I was terribly frightened. I was experiencing the most acute kind of animal panic. But I also experienced moments of elation, of tremendous intensity. I felt as if something fantastic was happening, as if I had embarked on a great adventure—it was the adventure of being ill and probably dying, and it *is* something extraordinary to become willing to die. I don't want to say it was a positive experience, because that sounds cheap, but of course it did have a positive side.

So your experience didn't at all "cancerize" your thought processes, so to speak.

No, because it was two weeks after I was told I had cancer that I cleaned out those ideas. The first thing I thought was: What did I do to deserve this? I've led the wrong life, I've been too repressed. Yes, I suffered a great grief five years ago and this must be the result of that intense depression.

Then I asked one of my doctors: "What do you think about the psychological side of cancer in terms of what causes it?" And he said to me, "Well, people have said a lot of funny things about diseases throughout the ages, and of course they never turned out to be true." I mean, he just dismissed it absolutely. So I then began to think about TB, and the argument of the book fell into place. And I decided that I was not going to be culpabilized. I have the same tendencies to feel guilty that everybody has, probably more than average, but I don't like it. Nietzsche was right about guilt, it's awful. I'd rather feel *ashamed.* That seems more objective and has to do with one's personal sense of honor.

In your essay about your trip to Vietnam, you write about the differences between shame and guilt cultures.

Well, obviously there is some overlap—one can feel ashamed of oneself because one hasn't met a certain standard. But people do feel guilty about being ill. I personally like to feel responsible. Whenever I find myself in a mess in my personal life, like being involved with the wrong person, or with my back to the wall in some way—the kind of things that happen to everybody—I always prefer to take responsibility myself rather than to say it's the other person's fault. I hate seeing myself as a victim. I'd rather say, Well, I chose to fall in love with this person who turned out to be a bastard. It was *my* choice, and I don't like blaming other people because it's so much easier to change oneself than to change other people. So it isn't that I don't like to take responsibility, but in my view, when you do get sick and have a drastic illness, it's like being hit by a car, and I don't think it makes much sense to worry about what made you ill. What does make sense is to be as rational as you can in seeking the right kind of treatment and to really want to live. There's no doubt that if you don't want to live you can be in complicity with the illness.

Job didn't feel guilty—he felt stubborn and angry.

I felt extremely stubborn. But I didn't feel angry, because there was nobody to feel angry at. You can't feel angry at nature. You can't feel angry at biology. We're all going to die—that's a very difficult thing to take in—and we all experience this process. It feels as if there's this person—in your head, mainly—trapped in this physiological stock that can only survive seventy- or eighty-plus years normally, in any kind of decent condition. It starts deteriorating at a certain point, and then for half of your life, if not more, you watch this material begin to fray. And there's nothing you can do about it. You're trapped inside it, and when it goes, you go. We all have that experience of ourselves. You ask people who are sixty or seventy years old, if you know them well, how old they feel, and they'll tell you they feel like they're fourteen . . . and then they look in the mirror and see this old face, and so they feel like a fourteen-year-old trapped in an old body! You *are* trapped in this perishable stuff. It's not only that it eventually gives out like a machine that's only designed to last so long, but it slowly deteriorates, and as the years go by you can see that it functions less well, the skin doesn't look so pretty, certain things come unhinged, and that's a very sad experience.

As Shakespeare put it: "Sans teeth, sans eyes, sans taste, sans everything."

Yes. Charles de Gaulle said old age is a shipwreck, and it's true.

What about all the philosophical and quasi-mystical attempts to overcome that duality? Right now, you've been speaking from an experiential, commonsense point of view.

I think the sense of oneself as a self trapped in something is impossible to get over. That's the origin of all dualisms — Platonic, Cartesian, or whatever. Even though we know it can't stand up to any kind of scientific analysis, there's no way we can be conscious and not have a sense of "I am in my body." Of course, you can try to come to terms with death and try to shift the axis of your activities to things that are less body-dependent as you get older, but your body neither is as attractive to other people nor does it function in the way that is pleasurable to you because it's frailer and somewhat deteriorating.

The traditional trajectory of a human life is that it would be more physical in the early part and more contemplative in the later part. But one has to remember that that's an option that's barely available, much less supported by society. And it also should be said that a lot of our ideas about what we can do at different ages and what age means are so arbitrary—as arbitrary as sexual stereotypes. I think that the young-old polarization and the male-female polarization are perhaps the two leading stereotypes that imprison people. The values associated with youth and with masculinity are considered to be the human norms, and anything else is taken to be at least less worthwhile or *inferior*. Old people have a terrific sense of inferiority. They're *embarrassed* to be old.

What you can do when you're young and what you can do when you're old is as arbitrary and without much basis as what you can do if you're a woman or what you can do if you're a man. People say all the time: "Oh, I can't do that. I'm sixty. I'm too old." Or "I can't do that. I'm twenty. I'm too young." Why? Who says so? In life you want to keep as many options open as possible, but of course you want to be able to be free to make real choices. I mean, I don't think you can have everything, and you need to make choices. Americans tend to think that *anything* is possible, and that's something I like about Americans [*laughing*], and in that respect I feel very American, but there does come a point when you have to acknowledge that you're no longer postponing something and that you really *have* made a choice.

And regarding those sexual stereotypes: the other night I was in a situation with David [Sontag's son David Rieff] when we went out to Vincennes University, where I was invited to attend a seminar, and then after the seminar, four people plus David and myself went out to have coffee. And it so happened that the four people from the seminar were all women. We sat down at the table, and one of the women said, in French, to David, "Oh, you poor guy, having to sit with five women!" And everybody laughed. And then I said to these women, who were all teachers at Vincennes, "Do you realize what you're saying and what a low opinion you have of yourselves?" I mean, can you imagine a situation in which a woman would sit down with five men and a man would say, "Oh, you poor thing, you have to sit with five men and we don't have another woman for you." She'd be *honored*.

I wonder what David thought of that remark.

I'm sure that if he had been asked about it, he probably would have just said, What else is new? [*laughing*] But in fact I know that he was overwhelmed by those women's lack of self-esteem, by the misogyny of women. And don't forget that these were professional women who probably would have called themselves feminists, and yet what they were expressing was quite involuntary.

The obverse, of course, would have been for the women to have said to David, "Why don't you leave!"

Yes, sure.

That also wouldn't have been an attractive response.

No, not at all. But I think, as we were saying before, you can find something very similar between young people and old people, since if a young person — man or woman — in his or her twenties would sit down with a bunch of people in their sixties or seventies, one of those persons might have said, What a pity you have to sit here with five old people, that must be boring for you! The point about women is or should be obvious, but people haven't said how awful and embarrassed and diminished and apologetic they feel about being old.

It's a fascinating coincidence that Simone de Beauvoir explores exactly those themes and subjects in her books The Coming of Age *and* The Second Sex.

Well, I think she's fabulous — people run her down all the time in France, but although I disagree with parts of *The Second Sex*, I think it's still the best feminist book up till now — she's way ahead of the so-called movement. And I also think she's the first person to really deal with what it's like to be old as a cultural phenomenon.

Kafka once said something to the effect that the healthy drive away the sick, but the sick drive away the healthy. So it operates in both directions, and when you have those polarities they then become reinforcing. So how does one escape from that trap?

Well, I think that anytime you have an extreme experience, you feel a certain kind of solidarity with other people who have that same experience. I know that ever since I became ill, I feel much more for people whom I come in contact with who have a physical handicap or who are ill. I feel sympathetic in a more profound way, and I don't avoid that situation. That's not to say that I was an unsympathetic person before, but I wasn't moved in the way that I am now. I didn't try to be as helpful as I do today.

You feel more compassionate.

Yes, because I can now really identify with that person and what it is to be helpless and not be able to manage and to be in pain. There's a world of bravery and gallantry that is so inspiring. But, of course, I also know some people who are ill who are extremely exhibitionistic and can be sadistic, using their illness to dominate people and to exploit them. I'm not saying that it necessarily *improves* you in any way to be ill—every conceivable kind of behavior is produced. But if you've always been healthy, then to have that experience puts you, as the Buddha says, into another connection with people that is more compassionate. It can do that—not necessarily—but it can. And without any effort.

In their Journal, *the Goncourt brothers wrote: "Sickness sensitizes man for observation, like a photographic plate." And this seems to be a particularly fascinating statement in light of some of the themes you explore in both* On Photography *and* Illness as Metaphor.

It *is* fascinating. Perhaps we should first of all observe the ways people in this culture have decided that sickness is laden with all kinds of spiritual values. And that's because they don't have any other means to prod or extract something from themselves. Everything in this society—in the way we live—conspires to eliminate anything other than the most banal level of feelings. There's no sense of the sacred or of some other state of transcendence that people have always talked about since the beginning of thought. There's been a collapse of the religious vocabularies that once described that *other* state. Perhaps the only way people can even imagine it now—and in a way it's such a pathetic substitute—is in terms of being well and being sick . . . like the difference between the sacred and the profane, or the human city and the City of God.

Now, there *is* a truth in the romanticization of illness. I'm not trying to say that to be ill is nothing but a helpless physical condition. Of course there are all sorts of values attached to it, and they're like free-floating values that come to rest there because they're *harmless* now. So we begin to think that something extraordinary happens to us psychologically or psychically or humanly when we're ill because we don't know any other way to provoke some more extreme state of consciousness. There's not only a human need for transcendence, there's a human *capacity* for transcendence and for more profound states of feeling and for a greater sensitivity, and this has always been described in religious terms in one way or another. All of these religious vocabularies collapsed, and in their place we now have our medical and psychiatric vocabularies. So for almost two centuries, people have been imputing to illness all kinds of spiritual or moral values. All you have to do is read further back to see the way sickness was once described: people were sick and they didn't consider it a calamity of either a greater or lesser kind, they didn't think that anything good was happening to them or that any great psychological changes were taking place because they were *ill*.

The reason they didn't have to pin it on illness is because they had all sorts of other situations that had been invented, institutionalized, and ritualized over the centuries in which these things could happen—for instance, fasting, or prayer, or suffering of a voluntary physical kind like martyrdom. And we today don't have much: the two things that spiritual values have become attached to since the collapse of religious faith are art and illness.

In Illness as Metaphor, *you write: "Theories that diseases are caused by mental states and can be cured by willpower are always an index of how much is not understood about the physical terrain of a disease."*

Starting in the eighteenth century with people like Mesmer in France, you have the birth of a kind of modern spiritualism with all kinds of movements, some of which called themselves religions, some of which called themselves forms of medical practice—Mesmer presented himself as a doctor, for instance. These movements denied the existence of illness and said that, essentially, it's all in your head. Or that it was something spiritual. Mesmerism, Christian Science, or the psychological theories of disease are really all the same thing, they all convert disease into something mental or immaterial, and they all deny the reality of disease.

For instance, one of the things I discovered hanging around in the world of the ill is that most people don't have any understanding or respect for science except of the most primitive kind, which is to say as magic. Science

has such a terrible reputation in our society as being something that only causes evil. Of course, anything can be used
badly, any achievement, understanding, or instrument can
be put to bad purposes. But I think that as awful as the medical profession is—as manipulative, as shallow, as corrupt,
as materialistic in the way that it operates in our society—
a person who is seriously ill has a much better chance of
being properly treated in a major medical center in a large
capital city than by going to a medicine man. It's not that
people can't be cured by the power of suggestion, but most
of us have more and more complicated kinds of consciousness, and we don't seem to respond to that as well as people do in simpler societies where traditional folk medicine
does provide real remedies. A lot of herbal medicine has a
clearly explainable scientific basis. One of the important
forms of chemotherapy, for instance, is something that's
found in plants that have been used as a treatment for cancer in many so-called primitive societies. But I do think
that scientific knowledge really exists and really is progres-
sive, and the body is an organism that can be studied and
deciphered. The discovery of the genetic code has been
the most important scientific discovery of our time and
will lead to many things, probably including a really work-
able treatment for most cancers. People know things now
in medicine that they didn't know one hundred years ago,
and what they know is true.

What about the notion that one is somehow responsible for one's disease—the kind of argument you hear from some of the followers of est [a group awareness training program developed by Werner Erhard]?

I want to feel as responsible as I possibly can. As I told you before, I hate feeling like a victim, which not only gives me no pleasure but also makes me feel very uncomfortable. Insofar as it's possible, and not crazy, I want to enlarge to the furthest extent possible my sense of my own autonomy, so that in friendship and love relationships I'm eager to take responsibility for both the good and the bad things. I don't want this attitude of "I was so wonderful and that person did me in." Even when it's sometimes true, I've managed to convince myself that I was at least co-responsible for bad things that have happened to me, because it actually makes me feel stronger and makes me feel that things could perhaps be different. So I sympathize a lot with that.

But there is a point, as you say, where these notions become delusions. If you're hit by a car, it's very likely that you're not responsible. If you get a physical illness, you're not responsible. There *are* such things as microbes and viruses and genetic weaknesses. I think this is a kind of demagogic idea in this society, an idea that is taking people away, or distracting them, from areas in which they really could take responsibility. And I'm very impressed by the

fact that all these ways of thinking are so anti-intellectual —
most of the people who are most impressed by the psychological theories of illness don't believe in science. One of
the notions of est is that you must not say *but*. You're supposed to eliminate *but* and qualifiers of that kind from your
discourse, you should always speak in the affirmative because whenever you say *but*, you're tying yourself into
some kind of knot, you're expressing a *not*, and therefore
you must just be able to talk in a way such that you'd never
say, "on the one hand, but on the other hand." But the very
nature of thinking is *but* . . .

Or, either.

Right. Or *either*. It's all those things.

*This may be an apocryphal story, but someone once told me
about a guy he'd met who was so opposed to either/or con-
structions and ways of thinking that he actually began to call
himself And/or!*

Of course those are tricks that are the equivalent of lo-
botomizing people, and I think that they're essentially
ways for you to become more selfish and egotistical so that
you can think only of your own pleasure and run rough-
shod over other people's needs, because if it's a question of

you or me, obviously you'd choose *you*. I think this simply gives people a sense of superiority or security in their lives, and that's such a ghastly simplification. And as I said before, I'm assuming that there is a physical basis for disease. Obviously, this wouldn't convince a Christian Scientist who says, "I just don't believe that disease or death is real." Such notions flourish about a particular disease when medicine or science can't give a convincing account of what causes it and, more important, can't furnish effective means of treatment.

Tuberculosis is particularly interesting because its cause was discovered in 1882, but the cure only in 1944. All that stuff of sending people to sanatoriums didn't do them any good at all. So the myths and fantasies about TB—*The Magic Mountain*'s it's-just-love-deferred, or Kafka's it's-really-my-mental-illness-connecting-itself-into-a-physical-thing—started to vanish when almost no one died of TB anymore. And if people discover what causes cancer but don't find the cure for it, then the myths about cancer will go on.

In your book, the TB metaphor gets away with murder, being extremely resonant and suggestive. You point out, for instance, that the metaphor's romanticization exemplified the promotion of the self as an image, that the literary and erotic attitudes known as "romantic agony" are derived from it, and that it "refined" and made more creative, and even fashion-

able, those afflicted with the disease. Whereas the cancer metaphor doesn't get away with murder, it is murder.

Cancer is a very big metaphor, and it's true that cancer doesn't have those contradictory applications. It truly is a metaphor for evil, and it's not *also* a metaphor for something positive, but it's one that has an enormous allure. So often when people talk about what they really hate or fear or want to condemn—as if they don't know how to express a sense of evil—a metaphor is the most available and attractive way of expressing a sense of disaster, of what is to be repudiated.

I wanted to ask you about the illustration you chose for the book cover of Illness as Metaphor. *It's a fifteenth-century engraving of the school of Mantegna that shows Hercules combating the Hydra. In Greek mythology, Hercules had to perform twelve labors in order to atone for his having murdered his wife and children, and his second labor was to kill this venomous, multiheaded water serpent. According to one symbolic interpretation, each of the labors was linked to one of the signs of the zodiac in order to confirm Hercules' character as a solar hero. And in this particular interpretation, the Hydra was associated with the sign of Cancer. When I read that and thought of the cover of your book, it kind of blew my mind.*

It blows my mind, too, because I knew nothing about the symbolism of Hercules' labors.

Having decided that I was going to choose the cover for my book, I looked at all kinds of images—all the obvious things, like Vesalius [Andreas Vesalius's *De Humani Corporis Fabrica*, the seven-volume sixteenth-century textbook of human anatomy] and a lot of medical prints, as well as color photographs that I have of wax anatomical models from a medical museum in Bologna. I was looking, looking, looking . . . and then when I saw this image, it just leaped off the page. I never did any research, and it never occurred to me to find out what that image meant—I didn't even know that it depicted one of the twelve labors of Hercules. My choice was purely intuitive and arbitrary, and I just knew that that was going to be the cover for my book.

Why did it appeal to you?

First of all, I thought the male figure was sensationally beautiful. I think our reactions are so sensual and ultimately kinetic. There's something infinitely moving in the representation of the human form when one shoulder is as high as or higher than the head—I think it represents something incredibly vulnerable and passionate and strong. I notice that whenever I see a drawing of someone whose head is down and who has one shoulder up, I feel a kind of *ache*. And then there's his cape and the way his mouth is open and the way the body is foreshortened. He's very young there and looks almost asleep . . . and there's something very erotic in the face, you can almost imagine that it's the look of someone coming. And you don't know where the eyes are really looking—it's almost as if they're turned inward. You've seen all of those images of Saint George and the Dragon—there's always that rigid, martial gesture, with Saint George's arm up and the sword ready to be thrust into the dragon. But although Hercules also has got his weapon raised, the Hydra is practically attacking *him*, and you feel as if he's not going to get that sword down fast enough before the serpent grabs him on his side. So what this image conveys to me is a combination of vulnerability and a sense of passion.

It's interesting that what you chose viscerally for your book cover does have this astrological connection and also symbolically suggests the idea of Hercules freeing himself in his quest for immortality.

I guess that the only connection I made in this regard with the Hydra is that these ideas about cancer are like Hydras— you lop off one head and it comes back.

What you say reminds me of Roland Barthes's phrase "the metaphor without breaks."

Yes. And you know, when I was finishing *Illness as Metaphor*, I suddenly had the sense that in this book I was also returning to the idea of "Against Interpretation," because in a way, that's what it says: Don't interpret illness. Don't make one thing into something else. I never meant that you shouldn't try to explain or understand something, but just don't say that the real meaning of *x* is *y*. Don't abandon the thing in itself, because the thing in itself really exists. Illness is illness.

By the way, there's one metaphor that I left out of the book. In the modern period, the things attributed to TB have been split off—the positive, romantic things being assigned to mental illness and all the negative things to cancer. But there is an intermediate metaphor, one that had a career as interesting as that of TB, and that is syphilis, because syphilis did have a positive side. Syphilis was not only something laden with a sense of guilt because of its association with illicit sexual activity and because it was so feared and so highly moralized, but it was also attached to mental illness. It is, in a way, the missing link between TB and what happened in the split: mental illness on one side and cancer on the other.

In the late nineteenth and early twentieth centuries,

somebody who acted very strangely and seemed to have attacks of euphoria—something that's suggested by the French word *exalté*—was thought to have syphilis. Parents would send their twenty-one-year-old sons to doctors so that they could be checked out for syphilis if they started talking a lot faster, couldn't sleep, and were full of activity and ideas and fantastic projects.

It sounds like speed.

Yes, exactly. Like a kind of speed. Because that kind of behavior was thought to be typical of a syphilitic person. You get that in Thomas Mann's *Doctor Faustus*—the idea that syphilis is the price paid to be a genius, and it does take on some of the same qualities once assigned to TB. Syphilis, of course, brings on madness and suffering and eventual death, but between the beginning and the end, something terrific happens to you. You kind of explode in your head and are capable of genius. Nietzsche, de Maupassant—all those people who had syphilis died of it. But they had those exalted mental states that were part of, or produced, genius. So syphilis also did have a romantic side as a disease of genius that gave you a decade or two of the most intense and frenetic mental activity before you collapsed into total madness. But of course that was as much a result of the fact that they were geniuses as the fact that they had syphilis. There's nothing, however, like that with regard to cancer.

But what about leukemia?

Yes, leukemia is the only part of the cancer metaphor pulling toward the romantic values. Insofar as cancer can be a romantic disease, it's leukemia.

With regard to its romantic aura, think of Erich Segal's Love Story *or of the film* Bobby Deerfield.

Right. But also think of the pianist Dinu Lipatti and his last recital at Besançon in 1950—and I'm sure you've heard the recording of that concert—when he was helped onto the stage, gave this transcendent performance, and then died two and a half months later. The death of Dinu Lipatti dying of leukemia was exactly like the death of Paganini dying of TB, who was bleeding onstage in all of his last performances. So yes, leukemia is the romantic form of cancer. And maybe that's because it's a form of cancer that isn't associated with a tumor—you can't have a tumor in your blood. There's not that sense of something growing inside of you . . . but in fact something *is* growing inside you, because in leukemia you have *nine* billion instead of *two* billion white blood cells—there's a multiplication of cells, but it doesn't take the form of a tumor, and there's no operation you can perform for it, and there's no idea of mutilation and amputation that's connected to the fear of cancer. So yes, perhaps I didn't mention leukemia enough in *Illness as Metaphor*.

In your book you did emphasize the romantic aspect of madness. Yet I have the sense that over the past few years, that particular notion of madness seems to have lost a lot of its glamorous cachet.

But don't you think that the ideas of R. D. Laing are basically accepted by a lot of people? That the mad person, after all, knows something that we don't know and has gone to some end of consciousness? There was recently a piece in the *New York Review of Books* by Nigel Dennis, who's one of the writers I most admire in the world, and he reviewed a book about the treatment of a little girl named Nadia who was about five years old [*Nadia: A Case of Extraordinary Drawing Ability in an Autistic Child*, by Lorna Selfe]. She was a brilliant artist—and that's rare for a talent that is, after all, in the hand—and could draw like Goya. She was from nowhere, she was just this little kid, but she was autistic. And the book was told by one of her psychologists who wrote about how they all discussed what they

should do with her, and they realized that if they cured her
they would probably wreck her gift. In the end they did
cure her, and she can't draw anymore. Nigel Dennis writes
about this and — in a way that I will only be able to say less
well — makes out a case for letting her be mad and letting
her go on drawing. Though no one is saying that it's better
to be mad, it's quite obvious that her madness was a function of her autism, and she could only maintain her gift
if she were in some way isolated, with the isolation that
madness brings. But Dennis asks, Isn't it more important
to have a great artist? And she already was a great artist.

*It's what Rilke said: "Don't take away my demons because
my angels will depart as well."*

Yes, and that's because the two things come together. This
is a case where somebody is autistic and has this gift, and if
you take away one, you take away the other. This is not a
situation where you believe that her gift comes from her
autism, it's simply that if you start tampering, you probably
can't just withdraw one and keep the other. In the book,
the psychologist said that they thought that it would be better for Nadia to have the company of her family, because of
course her family wasn't able to deal with her at all since
she was busy doing thousands of pages of drawings each
day. But Nigel Dennis comments that she *would* have had

company—she'd have had the company of artists!—and he makes the case for the fact that the world has very few great artists.

I suppose it's just that the seventies zeitgeist tends to be embarrassed about, or even derogatory toward, the kinds of ideas expressed by Nigel Dennis and by a lot of the notions that flourished a decade ago.

Let's talk about this decade-mongering, because I feel that there's something terrible about making the fifties and sixties and seventies into major constructs. They're myths. Now we have to invent some new concept for the eighties, and I'm very curious to find out what people are going to invent. It's so ideological, this decade talk.

The idea is that everything that was hoped for and attempted in the sixties basically hasn't worked and couldn't work out. But who says it won't work? Who says there's something wrong with people dropping out? I think the world should be safe for marginal people. One of the primary things that a good society should be about is to allow people to be marginal. What's so awful about countries that call themselves communist is that their point of view does not allow for dropouts or marginal people. I think that, one way or another, there should always be the possibility for people to sit around on the sidewalk, and one of the nice things that happened before was that a lot of people chose to be marginal and other people didn't seem to mind. I think we have to allow not only for marginal people and states of consciousness but also for the unusual or the deviant. I'm all for deviants. I also think, of course, that it would be pretty impossible for everybody to be deviant— obviously, most people have to choose some central form of existence. But instead of becoming more and more bureaucratic, standardized, oppressive, and authoritarian, why don't we allow more and more people to be free?

I agree. To me, being in the San Francisco Bay Area during the mid-1960s was what I imagine it must have been like to have lived in Apollinaire's Paris or Mayakovsky's Moscow, and I feel really fortunate to have been able to experience that place and time. But I sometimes think that it's no longer affordable to be marginal, and it somehow seems as if there are now only little out-of-time places around the world such as Banff or Goa or Ibiza where people are still trying to keep that earlier spirit alive.

Come on, you can still go to the Med [the Caffe Mediterraneum in Berkeley, California]! There are still people there on Telegraph Avenue, as there are on Rue St.-Andrédes-Arts. I think it's just that *you* have changed. You're ten years older, you're a freelance person committed to a lot of work, and there's nothing like work to perhaps make that other kind of life seem less attractive.

I myself don't think of myself as marginal because I don't particularly want to sit on the sidewalk and take drugs—I'm too restless and I don't want to calm my restlessness. On the contrary, I'd like to be *more* restless and have more energy and be more mobile. If I want to be marginal, I want to be marginal in the sense of attempting a great many things, none of which I ever really finish [*laughing*], but not to be marginal in the sense of *not* doing things because it's all a rat race. I *know* it's a rat race, but part of my efforts is to keep myself marginal in the sense of destroying what I've done or trying to do something else. As soon as I see one thing is working, I don't want to do that anymore.

What is essentially different in the seventies is that there isn't the illusion that a lot of people think the same as you do. I mean, one is restored to one's position as a freelance person, but I don't feel that I've changed what I think. All throughout the sixties, I was horrified by the anti-intellectualism of the movement and the hippies and the bright-thinking people whom I stood shoulder to shoulder with in various political situations. I couldn't stand how anti-intellectual they were, and I think people are *still* very anti-intellectual.

I remember that during the sixties, the writer and activist Paul Goodman used to go to lecture at universities and the students would be saying, Let's tear them down. And he'd say, no, there are wonderful things here, we should use them as a resource. And they considered him an old fogey. I gather you feel the way Goodman did.

Absolutely. The whole attack on professionalism—what else have we got but professionalism? I mean, trying to be good at what we do and trying to enlarge the possibilities of serious and satisfying work.

Someone once told me that you used to read a book a day.

I read an enormous amount and, in large part, quite mindlessly. I love to read the way people love to watch television, and I kind of nod out over it. If I'm depressed I pick up a book and I feel better.

As Emily Dickinson wrote: "Blossoms and books, those solaces of sorrow."

Yes. Reading is my entertainment, my distraction, my consolation, my little suicide. If I can't stand the world I just curl up with a book, and it's like a little spaceship that takes me away from everything. But my reading is not in any way systematic. I'm very lucky in that I read rapidly, and I suppose that compared to most people I'm a speed reader, which has its great advantages in that I can read a lot, but it also has its disadvantages because I don't dwell over anything, I just take it all in and let it cook somewhere. I'm much more ignorant than most people think. If you would ask me to explain what structuralism or semiology mean, I couldn't tell you. I could recall an image in a sentence of Barthes or get a sense of things, but I don't work it out. So I have these interests, but I also go to CBGB and do other things like that.

I really believe in history, and that's something people don't believe in anymore. I know that what we do and think is a historical creation. I have very few beliefs, but this is certainly a real belief: that most everything we think of as natural is historical and has roots—specifically in the late eighteenth and early nineteenth centuries, the so-called Romantic revolutionary period—and we're essentially still dealing with expectations and feelings that were formulated at that time, like ideas about happiness, individuality, radical social change, and pleasure. We were given a vocabulary that came into existence at a particular historical moment. So when I go to a Patti Smith concert at CBGB, I enjoy, participate, appreciate, and am tuned in better because I've read Nietzsche.

Or perhaps Antonin Artaud.

Well, yes, but that's something too close, you see. I mention Nietzsche because one hundred years ago he was talking about modern society, he was talking about modern nihilism in the 1870s. What would he think if he were alive in the 1970s? Because the 1870s was a time when so many things that have been destroyed were still intact.

But how do you think Patti Smith relates to this?

In the way she talks, the way she comes on, what she's trying to do, the kind of person she is. That's part of where we are culturally, and where we are culturally has these roots. There's no incompatibility between observing the world and being tuned into this electronic, multimedia, multi-tracked, McLuhanite world and enjoying what can be enjoyed. I love rock and roll. Rock and roll changed my life — I'm one of those people! [*laughing*] Rock and roll literally changed my life.

What rock and roll?

You'll laugh. It was Bill Haley and the Comets — I really had a revelation. I can't tell you how utterly cut off I was from popular music because, being a child in the 1940s, the only things I ever heard were crooners, and I loathed them, they meant absolutely nothing to me. And then I heard Johnnie Ray singing "Cry"—it was on a jukebox—and something happened to my skin. A few years later I discovered Bill Haley and the Comets, and then I went to England in 1957 as a student and heard some of those early groups that were influenced by Chuck Berry playing in cellars and clubs. You know, to tell you the truth, I think rock and roll is the reason I got divorced. I think it was Bill Haley and the Comets and Chuck Berry [*laughing*] that made me decide that I had to get a divorce and leave the academic world and start a new life.

It sure couldn't have been the lines "Get out in that kitchen and rattle those pots and pans / Well, roll my breakfast 'cause I'm a hungry man" in "Shake, Rattle, and Roll" that got to you!

Not at all [*laughing*]. It wasn't the words, it was the *music*. To put it very plainly: I heard a Dionysian sound, and just as in *The Bacchae*, I stood up and wanted to follow. I mean, I didn't know what I wanted to do—I wasn't going to go out and join a band—but I knew that it was like the last line in the famous Rilke poem ["Archaic Torso of Apollo"]: "You must change your life."

And I knew it viscerally. During the late fifties, I lived in a totally academic university world. Nobody knew anything, and I didn't know one single person I could share this with, and I didn't talk about it to anybody. I didn't say, Did you *hear* this music? The people I knew were talking about Schönberg. People say a lot of stupid things about the fifties, but what *was* true about that time was that there was this total separation between those who were tuned into popular culture and those who were involved in high culture. There was nobody I ever met who was interested in both, and I always was, and I used to do all sorts of things by myself because I couldn't share this with anybody else. But then, of course, all of that changed. And that's what was interesting about the sixties. But now because high culture is being liquidated, one wants to take a step backward and say, Whoa, wait a minute, Shakespeare is still the greatest writer who ever lived, let's not forget that.

You've referred to yourself as being, at one and same time, a "besotted aesthete" and an "obsessed moralist." Yet it seems that many people aren't aware of the moralist side of you. In your essay on Leni Riefenstahl and the nature of fascist art, you wrote: "Riefenstahl's films express longings whose romantic ideal is expressed in youth/rock culture, primal therapy, Laing's anti-psychology, Third World camp following, and belief in gurus and the occult." That covers a lot of ter-

ritory, and it seems to me that in other contexts you've been sympathetic to a number of aspects of the romantic ideal.

It seems to be quite convincing to argue that Buddhism is the highest spiritual moment of humanity. It seems clear to me that rock and roll is the greatest movement of popular music that's ever existed. If somebody asks me if I like rock and roll, I tell them that I *love* rock and roll. Or if you ask me if Buddhism is an incredible moment of human transcendence and profundity, I would say yes. But it's something else to talk about the way in which interest in Buddhism occurs in our society. It's one thing to listen to punk rock as music, and another to understand the whole S&M–necrophilia–Grand Guignol–*Night of the Living Dead–Texas Chainsaw Massacre* sensibility that feeds into that. On the one hand, you're talking about the cultural situation and the impulses people are getting from it, and on the other, you're talking about what the thing is. And I don't feel it's a contradiction. I'm certainly not going to give up on rock and roll. I'm not going to say that because kids are walking around in their vampire makeup or wearing swastikas therefore this music is no good, which is the square, conservative judgment that's so much in the ascendant now. That's easy to say because most people who make those judgments, of course, know nothing about the music, aren't attracted to it, and have never been moved viscerally or sensually or sexually by it. Any more than I want to give up on my admiration for Buddhism because of what's happened to it in California or Hawaii. Everything is always abused, and then one is always trying to disentangle things.

Now, I think that there *is* a fascist cultural impulse that's voracious. To take the traditional example, and it's the one that precedes all the examples we use from contemporary popular culture: Nietzsche. Nietzsche really was an inspiration for Nazism, and there are things in his writings that seem to prefigure and support the Nazi ideology.

But I'm not going to give up on him because of that, though I'm also not going to deny that things could be developed in that way.

Would you say that there is such a thing as a fascist sensibility?

Yes, I think there's a fascist sensibility that can plug into a lot of different things. Listen, rather early on, I became aware that it was there in a lot of the activities of the New Left. That was very disturbing, and it was a thing one didn't want to say too loudly in public in the late sixties or early seventies when the principal effort was to stop the American war in Vietnam. But it was very clear that a lot of the activities of the New Left were very far from democratic socialism and were deeply anti-intellectual, which I think of as part of the fascist impulse—anticultural and full of resentment and brutality and reflecting a kind of nihilism. There are things in the rhetoric of fascism that sound like the New Left. That is *not* to say, however, that the New Left is fascism, which is what all kinds of conservatives and reactionaries are prone to declare. But one has to be very alive to the fact that all of these things are not just objects but processes, and it's the human nature of our situation to be extremely complicated. There are contradictory impulses in everything, and you have to keep directing your attention to what is contradictory and try to sort these things out and to purify them.

When you were speaking before about the S&M-necrophiliac sensibility, I was reminded of your controversial essay "The Pornographic Imagination" and of your risk-taking exploration of that sensibility and imagination. But in that essay, you seem to be making what I think are some rather debatable arguments about the nature of extreme forms of sexual experience. I have to confess that I tend, perhaps naïvely, to agree with the psychoanalyst Wilhelm Reich's notion that masochistic and sadistic impulses are somatically rooted and are functions of characterological armoring and bioenergetic stasis. But in your essay, you state that "tamed as it may be, sexuality remains one of the demonic forces in human consciousness, pushing us at intervals close to taboo and dangerous desires, which range from the impulse to commit sud-

den arbitrary violence upon another person to the voluptuous
yearning for the extinction of one's consciousness, for death
itself."

Listen, I think there's one idea of Reich's that is a fantastic
contribution to psychology and therapy, and that is his idea
of character armor and the way in which emotions are
stored in the body as rigidity and antisexuality. He's absolutely right about that. But I think that he really didn't
understand the demonic in human nature and that he had
a picture of sexuality only as something wonderful. And of
course it can be, but it's also a very dark place and a theater
of the demonic.

*In your essay "Fascinating Fascism," you present a startling
formulation of the master scenario of the theater of S&M:
"The color is black, the material is leather, the seduction is
beauty, the justification is honesty, the aim is ecstasy, the
fantasy is death." I suppose I don't deeply understand this
because I haven't yet passed through those beckoning gates
of hell.*

I don't *deeply* understand it because it's not me, but I guess
I understand it more than you in the sense that I know it's
for real, and know that the reason that people can continue
to have an idea of sexuality simply as pleasure—in the most

desirable sense as contact, love, and sensuality—is that they don't go to the end of what sexuality is . . . and they probably shouldn't, of course, because one is playing with fire. And if one goes to the end, I think it's a much bigger and more anarchic thing than one imagines, and that's why throughout human history it's been the subject of so much regulation. I don't think people understand why there's been this problem of repression. I'd sort of turn it around and say that the reason most societies have been, to a considerable extent, repressive about sexuality is that people *have* understood that it can get out of control and be completely destructive.

In this regard, I can't help thinking of two of my favorite lines by William Blake: "Consider this, O mortal man, O worm of sixty winters / Consider Sexual Organization and hide thee in the dust."

Yes, there's something wrong with human sexuality [*laughing*]. You see, we're not animals. Now, there's nothing wrong with animal sexuality, but at the same time it *is* kind of awful because it's so purely physical and for the most part is so extremely disagreeable to the female. With the exception of some species like wolves, for instance, who have something more like a family life and tend to be monogamous, it's generally this crazy kind of disconnected, dissociated act that, as I said, is very unfavorable for the female and really does seem to be the reproductive urge and nothing more. Human sexuality, however, is something entirely different, but it didn't quite work out—in fact, I once described the human sexual capacity as being incorrectly designed. I mean, to move sexuality onto another plane whereby it becomes a psychological and emotional thing doesn't quite work—it only works when it's controlled or inhibited in some way. Did you see that movie by Nagisa Ôshima called *In the Realm of the Senses?*

I did, and I'm afraid that I'm never going to be able to forget it. There's no way you can forget the ending of that film when the woman strangles the man while they're making love and then cuts off his penis and writes the words "The Two of Us Forever" on her chest in blood.

You know, I think Ôshima's right. I think that's an authentic experience. Luckily it's given to very few people. But this is a perfect illustration of what happens when you don't have any breaks anymore. They went to the end, and the end is death.

When Wilhelm Reich writes about what happens when fascism takes ahold of this kind of destructive impulse, he ex-

*presses a different view of sexuality than I think you do. He
sees fascism as exploiting the frustrations of repressed sexual
desires, whereas it seems to me that you might say that because the sexual human organism is sick at its root, fascism
can easily exploit it. But I think that Reich would argue that
it can be exploited because in fact it is healthy and just can't
find a way to express itself in a healthy way. Do you see what
I mean?*

But I believe that that's true, too. I know people who have
very pleasurable, sensuous, nondestructive, non-S&M sexual lives. Not for a minute am I saying that that's not
possible. In fact, not only is it possible, it's desirable. I just
think the people who can do that don't take it to the limit,
and, as I said before, they shouldn't. But I don't agree with
Reich that fascism primarily comes out of sexual repression, though I do think that it had a very powerful sexual
rhetoric that was appealing to people.

*You once made the fascinating observation that the fad for
Nazi regalia, rather than affirming one's sense of individuality, is actually a response to "an oppressive freedom of choice
in sex" and also to "an unbearable degree of individuality."*

Yes, and I would extend that to the punk phenomenon as
well. But because people know that I like to go to some of

those concerts, they're always asking me how I can do that, exactly because of the Nazi regalia. But I don't think this is a rebirth of fascism but rather an expression of a desire for strong sensation in a nihilistic context. Our society is based on nihilism—television is nihilism. I mean, nihilism isn't some modernist invention of avant-garde artists. It's at the very heart of our culture.

We talked before about the drawing of Hercules and the Hydra that you chose for the front cover of Illness as Metaphor, *and I also wanted to ask you about the photograph and the lithograph that you used as the front and back covers for your book* On Photography. *The back cover is a cartoon by Honoré Daumier that shows the nineteenth-century French photographer Félix Nadar leaning out of a hot-air balloon to take an aerial photograph of the city of Paris below him. And this cartoon exemplifies what you describe as the photographer's role as an objective recorder, "note-taking on potentially everything in the world from every possible angle."*

Don't forget that this was, of course, a time before airplanes, and even a balloon was still a very rare means of locomotion. So this is a God's-eye view, and it looks rather dangerous—Nadar appears as if he could actually fall out of the balloon, which gives you a sense of how precarious his position is. He could have just as well crouched down, and I'm sure when he did go up in a balloon to take aerial photos, most of his body was below the rim of the basket. But the most striking thing about the image is the way Paris—the World—is represented. It has the word PHOTO-GRAPH written on all the buildings: so it's a photographer taking a picture of photography!

On the front cover is a photograph of a daguerreotype, and this image shows two persons holding *another* daguerreotype. In the Daumier lithograph, the photographer is taking a picture of a world that is transformed into . . . what? Photography. So the back cover lithograph and the front-cover photograph both indicate or intimate in image form something about the reflexive nature of photography.

With regard to the cover photograph, I was reminded of your statement that "art is the most general condition of the past in the present. To become past is, in one version, to become art." And you've also spoken about how the past itself gives to photography an artistic dimension. As I read this front-cover photograph, I see a man holding a daguerreotype and looking very moony and nostalgic about something that's already in the past, while the woman next to him is looking straight out at the camera into the future. It's such a suggestive and haunting image.

Absolutely. I looked at countless thousands of photographs as I was working on this material, and as I was flipping through a book, I came across this photograph and said, *That's* the cover of *On Photography*. It just leapt out at me, and I knew that it said in capsule form so much of what the book is about—the image is so rich. And it struck me right away how different these two people are. As you point out, the man who has this moony look is actually the one who is tightly holding the daguerreotype photo, while the woman is resting her right hand on the frame. You don't feel that she's really holding it, she's just uniting herself with him to make a composition because it was something they posed for, and she can look out because she's less connected with the picture. By virtue of his really *holding* the daguerreotype very close to his head, he becomes much more related to it, so that he can't look out in the same way. So I do see this difference in their two kinds of looks. I don't know why one assumes that they're a couple, because they could also be brother and sister, and those might be their parents in the daguerreotype.

I thought before that I might be "reading" too much into the photograph, using a literary expression to discuss a visual phenomenon.

Well, I think that we *do* speak of "reading" photographs. Again, it's a *metaphor*, and the notion of reading a photograph carries a great deal of baggage. But it's true that photographs repay a certain kind of attention and that you can see more and more in them. There are photographs I've looked at where suddenly I would see something that I realized I hadn't seen before. Obviously, I had seen it, in the sense that eye does take it all in, but I hadn't really because I hadn't concentrated on it.

In your book, you speak of the nature and main characteristics of photography with words like polymorphous, polyvalent, pluralistic, proliferating, dissociating, *and* consuming, *and you also identify it with an affluent, wasteful, and restless way of seeing the world. Over and over again, you use the following verbs with regard to photographs:* appropriate, package, possess, colonize, patronize, imprison, consume, collect, *and* aggress.

Yes, but also a lot of other words: *fascinate, haunt, entrance, inspire, delight.* But I'd especially like to go back to the word *aggress* that you mentioned and which is something that a lot of people have picked on. To me, to say that something is aggressive is in and of itself not a bad thing. Perhaps I thought that that was understood, and now I realize that *aggression* is a word that, quite hypocritically, people have

made very pejorative. I say hypocritically because this society is involved in colossal aggressions against nature and
all sorts of orders of being. I mean, to *live* is an aggression.
You're involved with aggressions on all levels when you
move around the world, you're occupying a space that
other people can't occupy, you're stepping on flora, fauna,
and little creatures as you walk. So there is a *normal* aggression that is part of the rhythm of living. I think there are
particular *heightenings* of a certain kind of characteristi-
cally modern forms of aggressiveness that are represented
in the use of a camera, as when you go up to someone and
say, Stand still, and you take that person's picture. These
are kinds of appropriations that people find very normal
and desirable because they have cameras, and when they
see something and want to take it home, they do so in the
form of a picture. They collect the world. But I don't want
to be understood as suggesting that it's photography that
introduced appropriation and collecting and aggressiveness, or that without it there would be none of these things
in the world. Of course I don't say that, but I have a feeling
sometimes that I'm *understood* to be saying that.

*But don't you think that you do identify photography with a
certain kind of consumer society.*

Oh, sure. Absolutely.

In your story "Project for a Trip to China" from your book I, etcetera, *you write: "Travel as accumulation. The colonialism of the soul, any soul, however well-intentioned." And in another story,"Unguided Tour," you declare: "I don't want to know more than I know, don't want to get more attached to [famous places] than I already am." In your essay "The Aesthetics of Silence," you observe that "an efficacious art work leaves silence in its wake." And in your famous essay "Against Interpretation," you remark: "To interpret is to impoverish, to deplete the world—in other to set up a shadow world of 'meanings.' It is to turn the world into this world. . . . The world, our world, is depleted, impoverished enough. Away with all duplicates of it, until we again experience more immediately what we have." It seems that throughout your work you've been talking about the same thing.*

Yes, it's the same thing, it's everywhere. But I didn't know this, I must tell you. I had no idea that I'd been saying the same thing since I started writing. It's amazing, but I almost don't want to think about it too much because something might happen to the material in my head. Most of what I do, contrary to what people think, is so intuitive and unpremeditated and not at all that kind of cerebral, calculating thing people imagine it to be. I'm just following my instincts and intuitions. See, I've always thought of the essays and the fiction as dealing with very different themes, and I've been irritated by carrying what I thought to be a double burden of two very different kinds of activities. It's only recently, because it's forced on my attention, that I've realized the extent to which the essays and the fictions share the same themes, make the same kinds of assertions or nonassertions. It's almost frightening to me to discover how unified they are.

The French film critic André Bazin believed photography could strip from the world "that spiritual dust and grime with which our eyes have covered it."

Sure, I talk about that in the fourth essay of *On Photography*—the notion that photography gives you new eyes, cleanses your vision.

And this connects with the idea of disburdening oneself.

I think that the idea of various notions of disburdenment is probably central to my work, beginning with my novel *The Benefactor*. I mean, what is it but a kind of ironic, comic story about a kind of Candide who, instead of looking for the best of all possible worlds, searches for some clear state of consciousness, for a way in which he could be properly disburdened. It's there also in those half-comic, half-straight reflections of this eccentric narrator. And I notice now that there are things about photography, too, in *The Benefactor.*

In On Photography, *you write: "Photography is the paradigm of an inherently equivocal connection between self and world," and you also point out that "there is an equivocation at the heart of all esthetic evaluations of photographs." I noted down a few of the equivocations you mention, and it's really quite a list: there's the equivocation between imperialism and democratization, between the deadening and arousing of conscience, between certifying and refusing experience, between radical criticism and easy irony, and between reality and image. So in* On Photography, *you've actually formulated a remarkable series of structural relationships.*

But that's exactly what I wanted to do. I love photographs. I don't take them but I look at them, I love them, I collect them, I'm fascinated by them . . . it's an old and very passionate interest. I got interested in writing about photography because I saw that it was this central activity that reflected all the complexities and contradictions and equivocations of this society. So those equivocations or contradictions or complexities are what it's about, that's the way we think. And what's interesting to me is that this activity, by which I mean both the taking of and the looking at pictures, encapsulates all those contradictions—I can't think of another activity where all the contradictions and equivocations are so built in. So *On Photography* is a case study in what it is to be living in the twentieth century in an advanced industrial consumer society.

Some photographers don't seem to be interested in this particular subject. Some of them even seem to feel aggressed upon, don't they?

Well, *On Photography* is not a book that any photographer would ever have written, but I think that all photographers know most of the things that are in the book. They either haven't formulated them or feel that it's not in their interest to talk about them. But when I talk to Henri Cartier-Bresson or Richard Avedon, who are two photographers I happen to know personally, they're aware of all that. Of course, they wouldn't write it, and it's not their business to do so. Some people have said to me, Well, you're not a photographer. Exactly. The point is that only someone who wasn't a photographer and who didn't have an investment in terms of the activity would have written this book. I have an investment in *looking* and getting pleasure from photographs, but if I also took pictures I could never have written *On Photography*.

*In your book you state that "the photographic world stands
in the same essentially inaccurate relation to the real world
as stills do to movies. Life is not about significant details,
illuminated in a flash, fixed forever. Photographs are." I once
read that the Mayans had a word for wisdom that meant
"the little flash," and mystics often talk about the flash of
insight or illumination. The critic George Steiner once wrote
about the flash of insight conveyed by the literary fragment
as it was used by writers such as Nietzsche and Wittgenstein,
and referred to both "its lightning certitude of immediacy and
the necessary incompletion of such immediacy," and high-
lighted its importance to the process of critical insight.*

First of all, those are very different levels of what happens.
There are flashes that I don't think are fragments. An epiphany is not a fragment. An orgasm is not a fragment. Of
course, there are things that are limited in time that are
extraordinarily intense and seem to take you into another
level of your consciousness or give you access to something
you didn't have before. The access might be, to use the
New Testament image, a strait gate, a very narrow place—
you do go through that and that's a kind of, if you will,
flash, and then it's something else. So the fact that the
thing might be small or brief doesn't necessarily mean it's
a flash. The question of fragments is another thing.

It seems as if the fragment is really the art form of our
time, and everybody who has reflected about art and thought

has had to deal with this problem. I heard Roland Barthes say recently that his whole effort now is to go beyond the fragment. But the question is: Can you? There's a reason why the fragment, starting with the Romantics, becomes the preeminent art form that allows for things to be more true, more authentic, more intense. There are privileged moments of pleasure and of insights, and some things can be more intense than other things because we live in many different places in our lives and consciousnesses. But the fact that you can distinguish a certain moment as being privileged—and not just because it's memorable but because it's *changed* you—doesn't mean that it's a fragment. It could mean that it's the culmination of everything that's gone before it. The fact that you can locate and separate things doesn't testify to their fragmentary character.

Your illuminating essay on Jean-Luc Godard's film Vivre sa vie *in fact uses a fragmentary-type structure, and by doing so suggests the radiance and plenitude of a movie that itself unfolds itself in a series of fragments.*

Well, I think there is something very honorable about the form of the fragment that points to the gaps, spaces, and silences between things. On the other hand, one could say that it's *literally* decadent—and not in the moral sense— in that it's the style of the end of an era, and by that I mean the end of a civilization or a tradition of thought or a sensibility. The fragment presupposes that one knows and has experienced a great deal, and it's decadent in that sense because you have to have all that stuff behind you so that you're making allusions and commenting on things without having to spell it all out. It's not an art form or a thought form of young cultures that need to make things very specific. But we know a lot and are aware of a multiplicity of perspectives, and the fragment is one way of acknowledging that.

I feel very restless with the essay form that uses a linear argument. I feel that I have to make things more sequential than they really are because my mind does jump around, and an argument appears to me much more like the spokes of a wheel than the links of a chain. And yet the nature of reading in a page form is that you start on the left, go down the page, move up to the right side, go down again, and turn the page. I can't think of a better way to do it, and I'm not suggesting that one should abandon the sequence of pages, but it's a way of getting something like what Joseph Frank many years ago called "spatial form." The question of fragments is very complicated.

Think of the ancient Greek fragments of Archilochos and Sappho that were actually remnants of what was once an original whole but whose reverberations still affect us so deeply.

And that's because we're sensitive to the fragment form. There are fragments that are created by the mutilations of history, and we have to assume that the words weren't written as fragments—they became fragments because things were lost. It seems to me that the Venus de Milo would never have become so famous if she had arms. It started in the eighteenth century when people saw the beauty of ruins. I suppose the love of the fragment first had to do with a certain sense of the pathos of history and with the ravages of time because what appeared to people in the form of fragments were works, parts of which had been lost or destroyed or dropped away. And now, of course, it's possible and indeed very persuasive for people to create work in the form of fragments. Just as when in the eighteenth century rich people put artificial ruins on their property, so fragments in the world of thought or art are like artificial ruins.

In a sense, so are photographs.

Yes, I think that photography comes in the form of fragments. The nature of the still photograph is that it has the mental status of a fragment. Of course, it's a thing complete in itself. But in relation to the passage of time, it becomes that telling fragment of what is left to us of the past: "Yes, we were so happy then, we were standing there, and you were very pretty, and I was wearing this, and look how young we were" . . . that kind of thing. I mean, when people take a photo, they don't do so in that spirit, but time changes photographs.

You assert that "it is in the nature of a photograph that it can never entirely transcend its subject as a painting can. Nor can a photograph ever transcend the visual itself, which is in some sense the ultimate aim of modernist painting." But what about, for example, the photographs that Alfred Stieglitz took of the summer skies with their billowing clouds at Lake George in upstate New York that convey the effulgence and radiance one finds in the paintings of Mark Rothko?

But that's because they're great photographs. You see, I mean those words very literally and not simply as words of commendation. Stieglitz is a great photographer, and what you feel when you look at those photographs is the response that you have to important works of art. By using the word *transcend*, I didn't mean that there aren't wonderful photographs or that they don't give you a sense of what you might get from a painting, but rather that the nature of the photographic enterprise is linked to representation in a way that painting is not. If you compare precisely Stieglitz to Rothko, you can say that you *get* that sense of radiance in Stieglitz, but it's still figurative.

Reference to subject matter can become very recessive as in the case of certain Turners and Monets or, in the case of Rothko, it can disappear altogether. But it doesn't seem to me that that's where the principal strength of photography lies. Of course, there are wonderful abstract photographs, but even abstract photographs have some reference. The photographs of a macroscopic or microscopic machine world of the Bauhaus tradition as represented by someone like Moholy-Nagy, for example, are only abstract in the sense that they're parts of a machine seen up close or simplified. But they're designed forms, and we still know that there is a world of objects like that.

In your essay "On Style," you wrote: "To speak of style is one way of speaking about the totality of art. Like all discourse about totalities, talk of a style must rely on metaphors. And metaphors mislead." What is your attitude toward metaphors generally?

I have to answer this in a more personal way. Ever since I began to think, I realized that the way I could understand things theoretically was to see their implications and their underlying metaphor or paradigm — that was a kind of understanding that was natural to me. When I first began to read philosophy when I was fourteen or fifteen, I remember that I'd be very struck by the metaphors, and I'd think,

Well, if you had another metaphor, it would come out differently. I've always had that kind of agnosticism about metaphors. Long before I had any ideas about it myself, I know that as soon as I found the metaphor, then that was a way of saying, Well, *that* is the source of the thought, but I could see how one could use another one. I know that there are a lot of theories about this, but I don't pay much attention to them because I'm much more following my instincts as a writer.

A lot of what interested me in modernist or avant-garde or experimental or what I just think of as good writing is a purification of metaphor. This stripped-down quality is what drew me to Beckett and Kafka. And when at one time I admired, more than I do now, French novelists like Robbe-Grillet, what appealed to me was their project, that idea of *not* having metaphors.

So when you talk of the purification of metaphors you mean the elimination of them.

In a way, yes, or at least an extreme skepticism towards them. Metaphors are central to thinking, but as you use them, you shouldn't believe them—you should know that they're a necessary fiction, or perhaps *not* a necessary fiction. I can't imagine any thought that doesn't have some implicit metaphors, but the fact that it does reveals its limits. And what attracts me is always a discourse that expresses that skepticism and goes beyond metaphors to something that is clean and transparent or that is, to use Barthes's phrase, zero degree writing. Of course you can also go in the absolute opposite direction, as James Joyce did, and just pack as much as you can into language, but then it isn't metaphor, you're just playing with language itself and all the different meanings a word can have, as in Joyce's *Finnegans Wake*. But I know that when I see a metaphor like, let's say, "The river went under the arches of a bridge like the fingers of a glove" . . . how's that one? [*laughing*]

Great!

Well, when I see one like that I feel—and it's a primitive and visceral feeling—as if I've been grabbed by the throat, I get a kind of short circuit in my head—I've got the river and I've got the glove, and one is interfering with the other. So I'm really talking about some fundamental kind of temperamental predilection on my part.

Now, in a way it sounds as if I'm ruling out all of poetry—look at Shakespeare's sonnets. It isn't that I'm against poetry—on the contrary, the two things I read most are poetry and art history. But insofar as there's something called prose and insofar as there's something called thinking, I think I go around and around the problem of what is a metaphor. It's not like a simile: if you say something is like something, well, okay, it's very clear what the differences are . . . although sometimes it's *not* so clear because poetry can be so compact. But when you say, for example, "illness is a curse," I see that as some kind of collapse of thinking—it's a way of stopping thinking and just freezing people in certain attitudes. The intellectual project for me is, in fact, one of criticism—in the profound sense of criticism—in that one is inevitably involved in constructing new metaphors because you have to use them to think. But at least you should be critical and skeptical of the ones you've inherited so that you're unclogging your thought, letting in air, and opening things out.

There's a beautiful metaphor I've always loved by the Mexican writer Octavio Paz that goes: "In the poem, being and the desire for being come to terms for an instant, like the fruit and the lips." To make the abstract so sensual is really a remarkable achievement.

Yes, I agree. But maybe the river-and-the-glove metaphor that I spoke about before bothers me because the river going under the bridge is *already* so sensual.

*It's ironical that the way you talk about metaphors suggests
that in some sense they function much as cancers do!*

[*Laughing*] Well, I certainly don't want to use cancer as a
metaphor. But perhaps you could say that a metaphor is
an impacted simile. When you say, for example, *it* is like
this, then your cards are on the table.

Look, I'm always thinking about what it is that's necessary to write. It's very hard for me to feel that all I want to
do is to tell stories because I know too much to just want
to do that. You can spend a thousand pages describing an
afternoon, but what do you leave out and what do you include? We're not naïve or bound by the conventions that
writers were bound by in the past. So in the stories in *I,
etcetera*, I was trying to do something else, something that
would give a kind of *necessity* to the material. The simplest
kind of necessity—it may be even in some ways the most
effective—is the form of the fable. A fable is not a metaphor, a fable is a story with a moral . . .

But perhaps a parable would be another example.

Yes, let's say a parable instead of a fable. The people I admire are ones who are struggling with the sense that what
one writes should in some way be irrefutable. And I find

that quality in Beckett, Kafka, Calvino, and Borges, as well as in a wonderful Hungarian writer named György Konrád.

What do you think of Nietzsche's statement that truth is only the solidification of old metaphors? He was talking about how stereotypes and clichés become the truth of the world.

But that's the truth in a very ironical sense. This may be my limitation—and it probably is—but I cannot understand the truth except as the negation of falsehood. I always discover what I think to be true by seeing that something else is false: the world is basically full of falsehood, and the truth is something carved out by the *rejection* of falsehood. In a way, the truth is quite empty, but it's already a fantastic liberation to be free of falsehood.

Take the question of women. The truth about women is that the whole system of patriarchal values, or whatever you want to call it, is false and oppressive. The truth is that that is *false*.

The patriarchal ethos has for centuries posited that women were the negation of men.

Well, *inferior*—the basic view is that women are better than children and less than men. They're grown-up children with the charm and attractiveness of children.

It always struck me that Cries and Whispers — *to use the title of Ingmar Bergman's film — is, in a sense, the world women have for so long been assigned to, not that of dialectical thinking.*

In our culture they've been assigned to the world of feeling, because the world of men is defined as being one of action, strength, executive ability, and a capacity for detachment, and therefore women become the repositories of feeling and sensitivity. The arts in our society are conceived of as basically feminine activities, but certainly they weren't in the past, and that's because men didn't previously define themselves so much in terms of the repression of women.

One of my oldest crusades is against the distinction between thought and feeling, which is really the basis of all anti-intellectual views: the heart and the head, thinking and feeling, fantasy and judgment . . . and I don't believe it's true. We have more or less the same bodies, but very different kinds of thoughts. I believe that we think much more with the instruments provided by our culture than we do with our bodies, and hence the much greater diversity of thought in the world. I have the impression that thinking is a form of feeling and that feeling is a form of thinking.

For instance, what I do results in books or a film, objects that are not *me* but that are transcriptions of something — they're words or images or whatever — and one imagines that

that is some purely intellectual process. But most everything I do seems to have as much to do with intuition as with reason. It isn't that love presupposes comprehension, but to love somebody is to be involved in all kinds of thoughts and judgments. That's what it is—there's an intellectual structure of physical desire, of lust. But the kind of thinking that makes a distinction between thought and feeling is just one of those forms of demagogy that causes lots of trouble for people by making them suspicious of things that they shouldn't be suspicious or complacent of.

For people to understand themselves in this way seems to be very destructive, and also very culpabilizing. These stereotypes of thought versus feeling, heart versus head, male versus female were invented at a time when people were convinced that the world was going in a certain direction— that is, toward technocracy, rationalization, science, and so on—but they were all invented as a defense against Romantic values.

In his poem "Élévation" from Les Fleurs du mal, *Baudelaire wrote: "Agile you move, O my mind, and as a strong swimmer / swoons on the wavy sea, gaily you cleave / the unfathomable vastness with ineffable, male, voluptuous joy." So here the poem connects thinking and feeling with a specifically "male" type of consciousness and sexuality. Recently, however, I came across an interview with the French writer Hélène Cixous in which, using another swimming image, she says: "To claim that writing doesn't betray sex differences is to regard it simply as a manufactured object. From the moment you admit that it springs from the entire body you have to admit that it transcribes a whole system of impulses, entirely different approaches to emotional expenditure and pleasure. . . . In writing, femininity produces a much greater impression of continuity than masculinity does. It's as though women had the faculty of remaining below the surface, coming up for air at very rare intervals. So obviously, the result is a text that leaves the reader very winded. But for me, that's completely in accord with feminine sensuality."*

Cixous began as a professor of English literature at the University of Paris, wrote a book on James Joyce, and now she's thought of as one of the leading women writers in France. Obviously, she considers herself to be a feminist. But I have to say that her statement doesn't make any sense to me. It's a fascinating contrast between Cixous and Baudelaire, but I think those images will yield anything you want them to. Baudelaire, after all, was the person who said that woman is natural, therefore abominable, and who had a very classic kind of nineteenth-century misogyny—the kind you find in Freud, i.e., women are nature and men are culture, as though women are this kind of slime that drags you down, and the spirit is always trying to escape from the flesh.

It's interesting that both of these French authors conceive of creative expression in gender-based terms—one swims and writes from a misogynist point of view, the other does so from a feminist point of view.

The culture of France is incredibly misogynistic in a way that just boggles the mind. I mean, the word *feminine*— not *effeminate*—but *feminine* is a pejorative word. To say that anything is *feminine* here, whether of work or of an activity or of a person—if that person is a woman and then only in a narrowly sexual sense—is always derogatory. Masculine means strong, feminine means weak.

But most of the French women I know are very strong people.

Well, this is also a country that had Joan of Arc! When I was once in India, I asked Indira Gandhi—knowing perfectly well what she was going to give me as an answer—if she thought that the fact that the head of state of India was a woman meant that people now had any different ideas about women, that perhaps they might think of women as being more competent, and she said, "My being prime minister doesn't mean anything, it just means that I'm an exception." So just because France, after all, produced a woman general doesn't mean that anybody else should be Joan of Arc—it's just that once in a while there are freaks.

But let's get back to what you brought up about what Hélène Cixous was saying. I'm very unhappy with the idea of labeling these things in sexual terms, so that, in fact, you'd have to say that Joyce is a feminine writer or working out of a feminine sexuality. I certainly think that there's *some* difference, not a lot, between masculine and feminine sensuality—obviously, a difference that everything in our culture conspires to make even bigger. There's probably some root difference just having to do with different physiologies and different sexual organs. But I don't believe there is such a thing as feminine or masculine writing. Cixous says that it has to be true because otherwise to write would just be to manufacture an object. In which case, and in that context—and if pushed to it—I'd say that writing *is* making objects. I'm comfortable with the old analogies that Plato and Aristotle used when they compared the poet to the carpenter.

If women have been conditioned to think that they ought to be writing out of their feelings, that the intellect is masculine, that thinking is this brutal and aggressive thing, then of course they're going to write different kinds of poems, prose, or whatever. But I don't see any reason why a woman can't write *anything* that a man writes, and vice versa.

It sounds in a way as if what Cixous is describing is a kind of stream of consciousness. And to me, it's an extremely good description of the novels of Claude Simon . . .

. . . or of Philippe Sollers or any number of other writers.

But in a very limited sense, it also could be said to be a good description of some of your own writing in that it posits an extremely intense development of material and ideas that sustains itself for quite long periods—and I think that On Photography *is a good example of that.*

But I think that so much that's good is an example of that. For a certain group of feminist writers and people who talk about these things, somebody like Hannah Arendt would be considered a male-identified intellectual. She happens to be a woman, but she's playing the man's game that starts with Plato and Aristotle and continues with Machiavelli and Thomas Hobbes and John Stuart Mill. She's the first woman political philosopher, but her game—its rules, discourse, references—is that of the tradition established with Plato's *Republic.* She never asked herself: "Since I'm a woman, shouldn't I be approaching these questions differently?" Indeed she didn't, and I don't think she should have. If I'm going to play chess, I don't think I should play differently because I'm a woman.

Obviously, that is a more rule-determined kind of game, but even if I'm a poet or a prose writer or a painter, it seems to me my choices have to do with all kinds of different traditions that I've become attached to, or of experiences I've had, *some* of which may have something to do with the fact that I'm a woman but need not at all be necessarily determinant. I think it's very oppressive to be asked to conform to the stereotype, exactly as a black writer might be asked to express black consciousness or only write about black material or reflect a black cultural sensibility. I don't want to be "ghettoized" any more than some black writers I know want to be ghettoized.

Before, however, you said that ill people have an attunement with one another. Also the old. You did talk about the male-female polarity as a kind of prison, so why shouldn't a woman, who feels she has been in that prison, wish to align herself with a certain kind of feminism?

Sure, I'm not against their doing it, but I would be sorry to see writing start to be sexually segregated. I've been in that situation. Let's say a film of mine is invited to a woman's film festival. Well, I don't refuse to send the film—on the contrary, I'm always glad when my films are shown, but it's only the accident of my being a woman that accounts for my film being included. But as regards my *work* as a filmmaker, I don't think that has anything to do with my being a woman—it has to do with *me*, and one of the things about me is that I'm a woman.

A feminist response to this might be that you act as if the revolution had already been won.

I don't believe that the revolution has been won, but I think it's just as useful for women to participate in traditional structures and enterprises, and to demonstrate that they're competent and that they can be airplane pilots and bank executives and generals, and a lot of things that I don't want to be and that I don't think are so great. But it's very good that women stake out their claims in these occupations. The attempt to set up a separate culture is a way of *not* seeking power, and I think women *have* to seek power. As I've said in the past, I don't think the emancipation of women is just a question of having equal rights. It's a question of having equal power, and how are they going to have that unless they participate in the structures that already exist?

I feel an intense loyalty to women, but it doesn't extend to giving my work only to feminist magazines because I also feel an intense loyalty to Western culture. In spite of the fact that it's so deeply compromised and corrupted by sexism, it's still what we have, and I feel that we have to work with this compromised thing, even if we *are* women, and make the necessary corrections and transformations.

I think that women should be proud of and identify with women who do things at a very high level of excellence, and not criticize them for not expressing a feminine sensibility or a feminine sense of sensuality. My idea is to just desegregate everything. The kind of feminist I am is to be an antisegregationist. And I don't think it's because I believe the battle has been won. I think it's fine if there are women's collectives doing things, but I don't believe that the *goal* is a creation or a vindication of feminine values. I think the goal is half the pie. I wouldn't establish or disestablish a principle of feminine culture or feminine sensibility or feminine sensuality. I think it would be nice if men would be more feminine and women more masculine. To me, that would be a more attractive world.

As Ray Davies sang in the Kinks' song "Lola": "Girls will be boys and boys will be girls / It's a mixed-up, muddled-up, shook-up world."

No intelligent or independent or active or passionate woman I know has not wanted to be a boy when she was a child. You wish you had been born a boy because then you get to climb trees, and when you grow up you can be a sailor . . . or some fantasy like that. When you're very little as a girl, you're always being told that you can't do things, and you wish you were a member of the sex that seems to have more liberty.

Most boys don't want to be girls because they understand from the age of about sixteen months that it's *better* to be a boy. Children want to be active, and activity in boys is encouraged—getting your clothes dirty and playing rough, and all that is repressed in girls. And when you get a little older you realize that the whole thing is based on either/or thinking, which now has certain fashionable names, like the androgyne or androgyny, but I don't think you have to give it a name like that because then it becomes the property of just one group of polemicists.

But what about the people in the world who feel as if they were born into the wrong body?

Well, talking about science again, I think that one of the great things is that for the first time in the history of the planet one has the possibility of changing one's sex.

The famous case of Jan Morris is interesting because here's the first person we know who's changed sex who was already an articulate person in the previous sex, and you can then actually compare the writing before and after. We actually have an account [Jan Morris's memoir

Conundrum] by this intelligent, literate person of what the sex change meant.

There will undoubtedly be other accounts in the future, but what many people have remarked about Jan Morris's change is that she really identifies with a very conventional idea of femininity—that when James Morris thought how he would like to be becoming Jan Morris, it was: I would like to dress like this, I would act like this, I would feel like this, and did so in terms that I think are conventional cultural stereotypes.

In the current issue of *Encounter* magazine, there's an article by Jan Morris about a trip to Venice that she recently took. [The article, "New Eyes in Venice," appeared in the June 1978 issue of *Encounter*.] Now, James Morris wrote a wonderful book about Venice twenty-five years ago, and here we have Jan Morris going to Venice twenty-five years later with the two youngest of her kids whom she was once the father of. And it's fantastic to compare the article and the book. I was in Venice just two weeks ago, and every time I go there—and I go all the time—I always have a little Venice kit that contains three or four books that I like to read when I'm there. I always take James Morris's book on Venice with me, and I read it again—so it was very fresh in my mind. And when I returned to Paris and bought the current issue of *Encounter*, there was Jan Morris's account. But it's so clearly an account written by a woman. I could not believe that a sex change produced that change in point of view—it's a *cultural* change that that person, by changing sex, has assented to.

What do you mean when you say that Jan Morris wrote that article like a woman?

Because she writes about her children all the time. The article is about how she went to Venice and took her two youngest children . . . and you think, okay, that's a beginning. But the whole article is about, Well, my son felt this way and my daughter felt that way, and it was such a pleasure to watch them enjoy Venice, I felt such a thrill seeing it through their eyes.

So you're not referring here to Hélène Cixous's underwater metaphor.

No, I mean that she writes like a mother.

So that's the difference?

Well, okay, but that's a role that's filled with feminine stereotypes. And I know that I do it myself—I'm a mother, and I have an adult child about whom I still feel, well, you know, it's so wonderful what he feels, I'm so interested in what he does. I talk about him more than any *father* of a twenty-five-year-old might, and I brag about him. Very often I feel more comfortable if he's in the center of situations, and I'm sort of watching because I take so much pride in the way he's turned out. These are conventional mother-woman attitudes.

But there are male mothers now, too.

Sure, but the point is: who says you should do that kind of thing? I don't believe it's biological, I think it's cultural. I just think it's so interesting because the phenomenon Morris is our first example of what I imagine is something that will become a real possibility.

I personally think that the way both James Morris and Jan Morris have written about cities is pretty remarkable. Jan Morris's recent essays about Los Angeles and Washington, D.C., that appeared in Rolling Stone *magazine are not only beautifully written but are also extremely witty and extraordinarily insightful. And I don't get the sense from them that she's writing about those places like a woman.*

No, no. I don't mean to make any judgment about Jan Morris's writing in general. But what I want to say is that here's an example of a person who's in her early fifties and who is a travel writer and who takes two of her children on a trip. And no man would write as Jan Morris wrote. James Morris could have taken his kids along and would not have written that way. And I think that's obeying the stereotypes. It's not that I'm *against* this recent article, but it just seems that depending on the sex you are or, in these unusual cases, the sex you have chosen—because for the first time that has become a possibility through medicine—you then assign yourself certain qualities, such that you say, I have this kind of sensuality, I have this kind of affective relationship to young people, I'm more protective and perhaps in some way more self-effacing because I'm a woman rather than a man. But *of course*, as you say, men could feel this way too.

In "Old Complaints Revisited," the narrator-protagonist is purposely never defined as being either male or female. In a recent interview, I. B. Singer asserted that "if you are going to write, let's say, a cosmopolitan novel and write just about a human being, you will never succeed. Because there isn't such a thing as 'just a human being.'" Your story, however, seems to disprove Singer's statement.

"Old Complaints Revisited" plays with the notion that it isn't so important to be specific, because the real specificity lies in the use of multiple references. In the same way, my story "Baby" plays with the notion that you can have a first-person-plural narrator, and it doesn't matter which is the mother and which is the father talking to the psychiatrist, because they talk as one. They're Siamese-twin parents.

What I really would have liked, of course—but grammar locks you into these stereotypes—would have been to be able to refer to the child as "it" instead of "he." But you can't because the conventions of grammar don't allow you to do it. I could do it as long as "Baby" was a baby. The sex of a baby is very indeterminate linguistically for the first few months. I remember that when David was born, my husband and I used to say, "The baby, how's the baby?" Because it wasn't "David" yet. I don't know whether it's during the third or fourth or sixth month, or maybe when the baby himself or herself begins to use language, that it becomes appropriate to use the name. But since I decided that the child in my story was supposed to be the child at all ages—babyhood, adolescence, early adulthood—I couldn't say "it." It would have been too odd, and I had to choose. So I made it a "he," but I hated doing so. I mean, why should it have been a he?

"Baby" is one of my more autobiographical stories, and it draws on incidents from my own childhood, from my son's childhood, and the rest is made up. So I could play both the victim child and the monster parent. I think I've been a good parent, but I know that parents are also monsters and are experienced correctly by children that way. They're so much bigger: when you're a small child, your parents are giants! So I had to face up to all those complicated feelings in a nonsimplified way—my feeling of victimization as a child, which every child understands, and my also having been a parent. And then just let those feelings run.

When you write, do you feel like a woman, a man, or just disembodied?

I find writing very desexualizing, which is one of its limitations. I don't eat, or I eat very irregularly and badly and skip meals, and I try to sleep as little as possible. My back hurts, my fingers hurt, I get headaches. And it even cuts sexual desire. I find that if I'm very interested in someone sexually and then embark on a writing project, there's pretty much a period of abstinence or chastity because I want all my energy to go into the writing. But that's the kind of writer I am. I'm totally undisciplined, and I just do it in periods of very long, intense, obsessional stretches.

In the past, you've talked about bad speech as being dissociated speech and of speech being dissociated from the body and therefore from feeling, and I imagine you'd say this would be true as it applies to writing as well. And you've talked about sensuous speech as an expressive instrument of the senses. How does this tally with what you were saying about your writing habits?

Well, it does very immediately because that's one of the things I've been trying to change in my own writing. I would like to learn how to write in a way that's less punishing to my body, and I'm beginning to do that. First of all, although I'm not in the same state of medical emergency that I was until recently—according to my doctors there's considerable optimism now—I still feel fragile, and I still reasonably worry about getting in bad shape physically in a way that I didn't before because I'd never been ill and thought that my body could take an unlimited amount of punishment and always bound back. So for medical reasons I don't want to write in the same way I did before because I'm afraid of becoming vulnerable or lowering my immunological responses. But I've also thought that changing the way I write would probably also be a very good thing for the writing, and I've had exactly that thought as you suggest.

The body is always there as a backlog, there are all these sensations—you don't have to fuck to imagine it or to have sexual fantasies: it's in the head, and the body is also in the head. But I'm now trying to imagine what it would be like to write and feel really comfortable. Suppose you were naked and wrapped yourself in velvet! Would you write differently? I think you would.

Do you write sitting on a chair and at a desk?

I tend to write first drafts lying on a bed, stretched out. Then, as soon as I have something to type out, I go to a desk and a wooden chair, and from then on it's all at the typewriter. How do you write?

At a desk with a fairly hard chair and lots of things scattered around.

But don't you think you'd write differently if you were all naked and wrapped in velvet? [*laughing*] There are all these stories about Goethe, or maybe it was Schiller, who used to write with his feet in warm water. And Wagner, who only composed in silk robes with incense and perfume in the room.

Haydn would supposedly wear a ceremonial wig when he composed.

I also remember hearing about someone who said he always got dressed up in his best clothes to write. I'm always wearing blue jeans, an old sweater, and sneakers.

Vladimir Nabokov would stand at a lectern and write his book on little index cards.

I can't imagine standing up to write. But in that sense, I think the body can be changed.

Do you think the style would change if the body changed?

I think so. Because one thing I've become aware of in my own writing is that I tend to repress images. Again, it's the idea that it is what it is and it's not something else. I do use images sometimes, but I have a certain resistance to it. I tend to write in a linear way.

I made a list of four adjectives that I thought might be said to define your writing style: lean, measured, unruffled, unadorned.

Of these, I certainly do connect with *unadorned*. And I think I've always had the idea that that was a good way to be. It seemed to me that what was perishable in a lot of writing was precisely its adornment, and that the style for eternity was an unadorned one. But the two writers in America who fascinate me the most are Elizabeth Hardwick and William Gass, and they couldn't be more opposite from me—as well as from each other—and both of them constantly use images and develop things out of images and sink them back into images.

Someone says: "The road is straight." Okay. And then: "The road is straight as a string." To me, there's a mind-boggling difference between those two statements. There's such a profound part of me that feels that "The road is straight" is all you need and all you should say, and anything else is just confusion. But I'm now starting to get more pleasure from writing that says "The road is straight as a string." Yet even so, saying "There's the road" and "There's the string"—really, what do they have to do with each other? So this still continues to bother me.

But to get back to what we were talking about before about how you might be interested in writing differently from the way you'd been doing previously.

Yes, I would like to write differently. I'd like to find a different kind of freedom from the freedom I have now. I do have certain freedoms as a writer, but there are others that I lack, and I'll only find them by practicing them. Kafka said that you can never be alone enough to write, and he was right.

Don't you think that the nervous system in some way determines one's writing style and that it's not just a matter of changing one's garments?

I think that there are things stronger than the nervous system. My nervous system is certainly different from the way it was twenty years ago, however. I've taken a very modest amount of psychedelic drugs throughout my adult life. Smoking grass—something I've done in a very modest amount—changed my nervous system. For instance, it helped me relax. That's a dumb thing to say, but it's true. I never really relaxed in the same way that I do now before I smoked grass, and I smoked grass for the first time when I was about twenty-two. I don't have to smoke grass to relax in that way, but I just got in contact with the part of me that could relax. I didn't know you were *supposed* to relax or that it was any good or that anything would come of it [*laughing*], I just didn't know how to be quiet in the same way. What I did learn from drugs was a certain kind of passivity that was good for me because I was very nervous. And I mean passivity in a good sense, in a Reichian sense, because I always had to be doing something.

I was a terribly restless child, and I was so irritated with being a child that I was just busy all the time. I was writing up a storm by the time I was eight or nine years old—I couldn't stand to be still. And when I started to smoke grass a little bit in my early twenties, just simply taking a deep breath allowed me to know something about what it was like to hibernate a little bit now and then. And that was a lesson that my nervous system learned. My ability to relax has just made my life a little better. I'm not as nervous, I don't perform as many wasteful motions, I can do things a little more smoothly—though I could probably have gotten this lesson from learning to play *billiards* rather than smoking pot [*laughing*]. But in fact it was something that was helpful to me. But it didn't change my style. That's why I say that I think that writing comes from something much stronger.

What I'm trying to say is that one writes out of many things. You write out of what you admire. But you can and do exhaust influences. When I was sixteen years old, my passions were Gerard Manley Hopkins and Djuna Barnes, among others. I now find it impossible to read either of those people, yet I can't say that I don't think that they're marvelous in their way. It's just that I've learned everything that I could possibly learn from them, and their writings are engraven in my head, I know them in my heart. I've totally absorbed them, so what's the point of reading them again? On the contrary, what I want to do is to get *away* from whatever I learned from those two writers.

I think the most natural thing is to assimilate something very strongly when you're young because it *is* so much part of you—one is so much more receptive at that point because you don't know anything, and you're so passionate to have a model. But I don't think it's any kind of Freudian thing the way Harold Bloom describes it, as if there's some sort of a murderous impulse to destroy your influences. I think you can just use influences *up* that are no longer useful to you, and that there's a natural impulse to contradict your influences and to try the alternatives. But if the kind of prose now that makes me salivate is by Elizabeth Hardwick and William Gass, it's precisely because twenty years ago I wouldn't have responded in that way. Twenty years ago I was responding to Kafka like that, but I think that I've learned everything I can learn from Kafka. It's exciting to me to subscribe to something that's foreign to my earlier taste—not in an unfriendly spirit with respect to the earlier work—but just because I need new blood and new nourishment and new inspiration. And because I like what I'm not, I like to try to learn what isn't me or what I don't know. I'm curious.

I remember reading Jane Austen and Stendhal when I was in high school, but they just passed me by. And then I read them years later and was bowled over.

What you say isn't wrong. I, too, read *Pride and Prejudice* and *The Red and the Black* when I was in my teens and thought, What's so great about them? And then I read them again in my early thirties and thought they were the greatest thing. I quite agree that there are certain kinds of fiction that demand that you have more experience before you can appreciate them. However, two years ago, I reread *The Brothers Karamazov* and was just as thrilled, perhaps even more so, than I had been when I read it in my teens. I mean, it is *the* most thrilling, passionate, inspiring, exalted work . . . I was flying for weeks after reading it. I thought: This is unbelievable, now I know why I should live! I hadn't read it in so many years and I felt *exactly* the same as when I read it when I was seventeen. I think that *The Brothers Karamazov* is a book that you can read at any age and always feel that it's giving you something. But then there's, say, *The Red and the Black* or *The Golden Bowl* that you have to be an adult to read.

I read and was mesmerized by The Golden Bowl *when I was in college, but perhaps, like you, I may have inhaled something once too often because I'm not sure that I could focus enough now to reread that novel.*

Have you read Henry James's *The Princess Casamassima?* It's great, you should read it—it's really all about the 1960s!

But the point is that when you join this world, that is, the world that cares about such things, then it's like you're making yourself new dishes all the time, you learn how to cook in a different way, and then you go on a binge where you want this or that. I do think, however, that you can exhaust something in yourself, but you can always come back to it, and so one should never make these definitive judgments . . . though, as I said, I think that there are certain things that are really part of your childhood that you can never recapture.

Was there a particular book that you read when you were young that made you want to become a writer?

The book that made me want to become a writer was *Martin Eden* by Jack London—and it had a suicide at the end! I read it when I was thirteen. I couldn't possibly have the same thrill reading that novel today—Jack London isn't a satisfying enough writer for an adult person living now.

What was the first book that—vocational interest aside— really thrilled you?

It was the biography of Madame Curie by her daughter, Eve, which was a very famous book in the early 1940s—I must have been seven years old when I read it—maybe even earlier, when I was six.

You read books at six years old?

Yes, I started reading when I was three. And the first novel that affected me was *Les Misérables*—I cried and sobbed and wailed. When you're a reading child, you just read the books that are around the house. When I was about thirteen, it was Mann and Joyce and Eliot and Kafka and Gide—mostly Europeans. I didn't discover American literature until much later. I discovered a lot of writers in the Modern Library editions, which were sold in a Hallmark greeting-card store, and I used to save up my allowance and would buy them all. I even bought real lemons like Adam Smith's *The Wealth of Nations* [*laughing*]. I thought *everything* in the Modern Library must be great.

But when you went to high school you must have had to read books of much thinner gruel than the ones you just mentioned. When I was in high school everyone had to read George Eliot's Silas Marner.

So did I. I went to high school at the end of the 1940s and college in the early 1950s, and I'm ten years older than

you, but I'm sure that our high school curriculums were
pretty much the same.

*And you were teaching at Columbia College in the early
1960s when I was an undergraduate there.*

The years I taught at Columbia were fabulous, and I feel
very nostalgic for all that. I taught the Humanities and
Contemporary Civilization courses, so I had to read, for
instance, the *Iliad* every year. A lot of people ask me where
I find all of my references. Well, a lot of them I really do
know by heart because I taught the books they come from
for ten years.

When I was writing *Illness as Metaphor,* I didn't have
to look very much up because I remembered the plague
in Book Two of the *Iliad* and the Athenian plague in
Thucydides and the plague of Florence in Boccaccio, and
I became aware of how *unromantic* disease was considered
until the Romantic period. In those earlier books, disease
wasn't talked about as a psychic condition or as an apoca-
lyptic destiny—it was all about how it could be controlled,
managed, and rationally handled. And when I did start to
look, I couldn't find what seemed to be a modern use of
the disease metaphor before the mid-eighteenth century—
this notion of what disease could mean as an image of the
most extreme forms of the human condition.

But you can duplicate that development with many other ideas as well. There is a much more matter-of-fact view, say, of what we think sexuality is—everything we assign to it, all the values that it's the bearer of—before the modern period. I don't mean that they didn't care about it before then, but they weren't "romantic" about it in the sense of *in love*. I should say, however, that I don't think that being in love was invented by Provençal troubadours— I think there was a very extraordinary *flowering* of the idea of love so that it became very central and even institutionalized. That's a version of it, but there are many examples of erotic and romantic passion to be found in ancient and Oriental literature, for example. There's romantic love in Lady Murasaki's *The Tale of Genji*. I mean, people knew what it was like to be obsessed with another human being.

Regarding illness and love, I've often thought that, in their different ways, Thomas Mann's The Magic Mountain *and Italo Svevo's* The Confessions of Zeno *might both be seen as being about illness and love—the latter novel being a more insouciant and ironic antidote to the weight and portentousness of the former. Now, you've written about illness, but you haven't yet written about love.*

I would love to! But it takes courage to write about love because then you seem to be writing about yourself and one feels embarrassed, as if people will know something about you that you don't want them to know, and also because you want to be private in some way. Even if it's not true that I'm writing about myself, people will take it that that's what I'm doing, so I'm shy about it. But in fact I've been taking notes on an essay on love for many years. It's an old, old passion.

It's interesting that you mention shyness since you seem much less shy now than when I first met you in the early 1960s.

Yes, that's true.

When I recently reread your essay "Trip to Hanoi," I came across the lines: "I long for someone to be indiscreet here, to talk about his personal life, his emotions. To be carried away by 'feeling.'" And in the second part of the essay you begin to comprehend North Vietnam as if it were a previously opaque work of art that had now become transparent to you. And you understood it better as a work of art.

The reason why I waited until the second part of the essay to write what I did was because I felt it was important to acknowledge that the Vietnamese are different from us. I don't like this liberal family-of-man idea that we're really all the same. I think there really *are* cultural differences, and it's very important to be sensitive to those things. So I was no longer fighting for them to somehow come across and give something that I would recognize as a generous way of being with me because their way of expressing generosity was different from mine. They have their own tradition of behaving and speaking, and what they mean by intimacy is not what we mean by it. It seemed like learning a kind of respect for the world. The world is complicated, and it can't all be reduced to the way you think it should be.

You mentioned in this essay that you had just recently visited Cuba, and the Cubans were much more like us—manic, intimate, talkative—and that the Vietnamese were much more formal, measured, and controlled. To me, it seemed as if you were describing the difference between a film by, say, Marcel Pagnol or Jean Renoir and one by Robert Bresson. If these two societies were movies, you would probably have accepted both immediately.

Absolutely right, you're on to something that's very central to me. Of *course*, I'm much more provincial in my life than in the way I understand what is represented as art, which I'm more ecumenical about and more respectful of differences. And sure, I have a much narrower style. I really do like intimacy—intimacy of a Jewish kind, to put it in a code way. I like people who can talk a lot, who talk about themselves, who are warm and physically demonstrative. But I don't have to live in a Bresson or a Pagnol film, and I do have to live in my life and overcome my own limitations.

So let's say I'm more provincial or more local or more regional in my taste. It doesn't seem to be wrong. I mean, I don't want to be detached such that I would say that it doesn't matter how people are, because in fact I can appreciate people *however* they are. But my friends are mostly demonstrative people since that's something I like. I'm a little bit inhibited myself, so I like very much to be surrounded and close to people who aren't as inhibited in the way that I am because it draws me out, and that makes me feel good. And that's because it's my one and only life. But when I'm thinking about films or anything else, I'm thinking about the world, and then I'm perfectly comfortable with the idea that there should be some people doing it like this and other people doing it like that.

When you think about love as a subject, also a feeling, do you do so in the open way you appreciate films, or the reticent and slightly more narrow way you say you live your life?

The real change for me was that Vietnam essay, because that's the first time I ever wrote about myself at *all*—even though very timidly—and as I was doing it, it felt like a terrific sacrifice. I thought, Boy, I really do hate this war, and I'm willing to do this to contribute my tiny effort. But I did it as a conscious sacrifice. I thought, I don't want to write about myself, I just want to write about *them*. But when I realized that the best way that *I* could write about them *was* to include myself, then it was like a sacrifice. And it changed me. I realized I could have a certain freedom as a writer, which I never thought I even wanted, and therefore I have gingerly begun to explore that freedom in some of my stories that are autobiographical.

You did say that "an event that makes new feelings conscious is always the most important experience a person could have." And you also said: "It is not simple to be able to love calmly, to trust without ambivalence, to hope without self-mockery, to act courageously, to perform arduous tasks with unlimited resources of energy." When I read that, I felt as moved as I was when I watched Charlie Chaplin's great humanistic speech that concludes his film The Great Dictator.

That's what I would like for myself, but it's so difficult. The thing is that consciousness is such an incredible instrument, because as soon as you do become conscious of everything, then you're immediately conscious of something more. And as soon as you formulate an ideal for yourself, you see the limits of that ideal.

The statement of yours that I just quoted almost sounds as if it could have come out of Plutarch or Confucius, when heroic feelings and actions were considered the ideal way of being in the world.

I'm very attached to the idea of noble conduct. Words like *nobility* sound very strange to us now, and they sound snobbish, to say the least.

In "Trip to Hanoi," you write about the self-immolation of Norman Morrison. [To protest the United States involvement in the Vietnam War, the thirty-one-year-old Baltimore Quaker immolated himself below the Pentagon office of Secretary of Defense Robert S. McNamara in 1965.] And in that essay, you suggest that the Vietnamese viewed it not in terms of "practical efficacy" but rather in terms of the "moral success of his deed, its completeness as an act of self-transcendence." Strangely, that's what you were writing about in your essay on the aesthetics of silence, and I felt that in your Vietnam essay, art and life were somehow coming together a bit.

Well, I think they are. And in my illness book, they come together in a certain way, too, because it's a product of a very passionate experience. The place where I most hope they come together is in my fiction, and when I had to proofread the stories from *I, etcetera,* I was struck by the fact that they seemed to me as a *reader,* not as the writer of them, to have a theme in common, which is the search for self-transcendence, the enterprise of trying to become a different or a better or a nobler or a more moral person— in the sense that anything that one desires and honors has therefore a moral character because it takes on the quality of an art or an imperative or a goal or an ideal.

I wanted to speak to you about your stories later. But to re-turn to the idea of reticence versus openness . . .

It's so complicated because I do have—and I don't know whether it's any good as an idea—but I do have in my head an idea about being a child and being an adult. I turn those notions around and around in my head, and sometimes I think, there's no difference, this is a completely artificial distinction. Just because we get older and our skins get more leathery, so what? Who cares? What does it matter what age you are? We shouldn't try to impose any idea about what we should do that depends on whether we feel something is childlike or adultlike. And I have fantasies about childhood—not the childhood that I personally had but the values represented in the child's openness and innocence and vulnerability and sensitivity to things—and I think, how terrible that we don't preserve those qualities as adults.

So I have all these notions, along with completely contradictory ones that I'm always wrestling with. In fact, just this morning, when I was at the hospital, a friend came with me and somehow our conversation, while I was waiting to be seen by the doctor, turned precisely on this theme. I was saying, "Well, I'm an *adult*. I should behave like *this*." And my idea of adult behavior in *that* context was that I should be independent, I should be autonomous, and I shouldn't be afraid. So adulthood in that context represented very positive values—nothing like the romantic loss of imagination or the sense of drying up or petrifying. No, adulthood meant freedom, autonomy, courage, daring, alertness, self-sufficiency. I want to get *rid* of the child in myself.

I'm trying to say that I think our ideas of love are terribly bound up in our ambivalence about these two conditions— the positive and negative valuations of childhood, the positive and negative valuations of adulthood. And I think that, for many people, love signifies a return to values that are represented by childhood and that seem censored by the dried-up, mechanized, adult kinds of coercions of work and rules and responsibilities and impersonality. I mean, love is sensuality and play and irresponsibility and hedonism and being silly, and it gets to be thought of in terms of dependence and becoming weaker and getting into some kind of emotional slavery and treating the loved one as some kind of parent figure or sibling. You reproduce a part of what you were as a child when you weren't free and were completely dependent on your parents, particularly your mother.

We ask everything of love. We ask it to be anarchic. We ask it to be the glue that holds the family together, that allows society to be orderly and allows all kinds of material processes to be transmitted from one generation to another. But I think that the connection between love and sex is very mysterious. Part of the modern ideology of love is to assume that love and sex always go together. They can, I suppose, but I think rather to the detriment of either one or the other. And probably the greatest problem for human beings is that they just *don't*. And why do people *want* to be in love? That's really interesting. Partly, they want to be in love the way you want to go on a roller coaster again— even knowing you're going to have your heart broken. What fascinates me about love is what it has to do with all the cultural expectations and the values that have been put into it. I've always been amazed by the people who say, "I fell in love, I was madly, passionately in love, and I had this affair." And then a lot of stuff is described and you ask, "How long did it last?" And the person will say, "A week, I just couldn't stand him or her."

I've never been in love for less than a couple of years. I've been in love very few times in my life, but whenever I've been in love, it's something that's gone on and on and ended up—usually, of course—in some disaster. But I don't know what it means to be in love for a week. When I say I've been in love, that means that I've actually had a whole life with that person: we've lived together, we've been lovers, we've traveled, we've done things. I've never been in love with anybody I haven't slept with, but I know lots of people who say they've been in love with someone they haven't slept with. To me, what they're saying is: "I was attracted to somebody, I had a fantasy, and in a week the fantasy was over." But I know I'm wrong, because it's probably just a limit on my own imagination.

What about platonic love?

Of course, I have loved people passionately whom I wouldn't have slept with for anything, but I think that's something else. That's friendship-love, which can be a tremendously passionate emotion, and it can be tender and involve a desire to hug or whatever. But it certainly doesn't mean you want to take off your clothes with that person.

But certain friendships can be erotic.

Oh, I think friendship is very erotic, but it isn't necessarily sexual. I think all my relationships are erotic: I can't imagine being fond of somebody I don't want to touch or hug, so therefore there's always an erotic aspect to some extent. I don't know, maybe I'm again speaking out of my own sexuality, but I'm not attracted to that many people.

What do you think about Stendhal's theories of love?

I'm fascinated by his book *On Love* because it's one of the few works that we have on the subject, but I think he was so much involved with who people were . . . you know, this *was* the countess of such and such, and here she was in her clothes, and there she was in her drawing room, and there she was with her husband, and there with the ambassador, etcetera. Don't you feel you're turned on by people who are famous? Isn't that an erotic thing for you?

Not really, because I'm more attracted to people who are childlike, and anyone can be like that.

A famous person is *always* eager to tell you how he or she is really a vulnerable little child, haven't you noticed?

[*laughing*] They're so tired of being treated as formidable that they'll tell you quicker than anybody else.

You don't do that, and you're certainly formidable.

Yes, I do, but we don't know each other in that way. With people I want to get close to, I immediately try to explain that I'm just like a child. I feel a pressure to do it because I want a creatural relationship with them. I mean, you want to stop talking. This isn't any sort of grand metaphysical idea, but I do think that there are certain things that can only happen in silence between people, and if you're well known, people expect you to be performing or talking all the time or displaying your personality. I meet a lot of people who know who *I* am before I know who *they* are. So if a person interests me as a friend or lover or companion or pal, I *want* to introduce them to a creatural, silent person whom they don't feel nervous about . . . and I think that's natural. I like the silence that's transparent so that another person can see behind it. And I also don't want to do the thing that I notice some people do—particularly smart people—which is to completely split off, and say, "Well, don't pay any attention to these books I write . . . it's just little me." They're so eager to *placate* just to make sure that other people won't be intimidated by them, but by doing that, they're really denying who they are. And by doing that, they put the work in a corner and talk instead about wine and food and the weather because there's that sense that the work is something else and can't be shared. But I would rather talk about what interests me and not pretend to be simpler than I am because then you've won the affection of somebody on a false basis.

The writer Paul Goodman often spoke about his being attracted to boys who weren't interested in his concerns at all, and what attracted him was simply their animal grace.

I wish I could feel that . . . but there's that famous problem of breakfast.

What problem is that?

The problem about what you do the next morning. What do you talk about? I mean, here you have this revelation: you've spent the night with somebody, you're having breakfast together, and you realize that this person is only interesting to you sexually and that neither of you has anything in common. What do you do?

*Perhaps depart before the break of dawn! But actually I try
to avoid those kinds of nights and mornings.*

As a man, you've been told that that's part of male sexuality, that it's okay to have a relationship that's purely sexual.
But women aren't told that. If I find myself at breakfast with
an idiot, I feel embarrassed—although I don't think that I
should be—and I *also* feel—and that's part of the feminine
conditioning—that I've been exploitative. And then I think,
"Well, men do that with women and they don't feel that,"
but I can't help feeling that I'm slumming. Male sexuality
has been *built* on slumming. But instead of my thinking:
I'm slumming, good for me, it's okay, why not?—though
obviously I'd prefer a world in which no one was doing
that—I feel embarrassed, and I don't respect my embar-
rassment. I think that women, culturally, exercise an inhib-
iting force on men sexually. No heterosexual man can be
as promiscuous as a homosexual man, because he still has
to deal with women, who demand a little more than just
two and a half minutes someplace.

They might even want breakfast in the morning!

They might even want breakfast in the morning [*laughing*]. Sex is a habit like anything else, and you can get used

to a certain quantity of absolutely impersonal, easily procurable sex that lasts two and a half minutes. I think that the sexual impulse is infinitely malleable. It seems unlikely that people don't go through periods of general withdrawal from and resurgence of sexual feeling. So I think that that incessant pursuit isn't about sex, it's about power. Think of all the ways in which sex is fed by the impulse to be powerful, and it sometimes seems to be a culturally sanctioned way of combating feelings of insecurity, unworthiness, or unattractiveness.

So do you think that, in a way, sexuality can be seen as a kind of metaphor?

I don't think sexuality is a metaphor, but it's an activity that's been invested with a whole range of values that it itself doesn't necessarily invite. It can accommodate them, but it's become this tremendously overdetermined activity—it's overloaded with other values, other forms of affirmation and destruction that you're declaring when you engage in a sexual act—whom you engage with, what kind of person it is—and when you try to understand why people run away from it, why they seek it in the form in which they want it, the way they connect it with love. It's this tremendously elaborate rhetoric, and we've been instructed that it's in some way the central or *only* natural activity of our lives . . . and certainly that's nonsense. It's very hard to imagine what natural sexuality could be. I don't think that *natural* sexuality is available to any of us. I think it has to mean different things at different times in our lives.

One family therapist stated that there are either symmetrical or complementary relationships—the marriage of true minds or the marriage of dependency, so to speak.

But I think that that typology is just ridiculous because by those standards there must be one percent of one percent of one percent of symmetrical relationships in the world. And those ways of talking about relationships are so ahistorical. All these ideas that we have about the family and love and relationships are only a couple hundred years old. You know, people have this terrible metaphor about a relationship *working*—as if a relationship is a machine. We're filled with this imagery and these sorts of expectations. I mean, do these family therapists talk about the built-in inequalities that are orchestrated by the culture concerning male and female and older and younger persons? What does it mean to have an equal relationship between a man and a woman in this society? Most people would be satisfied with something that is not equal at all. You talked about "the marriage of true minds," but one mind is staying at home while the other mind is going to the office.

What about women who are in between that? What about yourself?

I was lucky enough to have a child and be married when I was very young. I did it and now I don't have to do it anymore. But that's not an example. I chose not to be married anymore, and then I already had a child—so I wasn't going to miss out on this great experience of being a mother—and then I decided to live a freelance life, which has a lot of insecurities and unpleasantness and anxiety and frustration and involves long periods of chastity. And I thought that that's what I wanted . . . but it's not really a model, it's just my own solution, and I only justify it to myself because of my life projects.

Was this a conscious choice?

No, but I did have the idea that I'd like to have several lives, and it's very hard to have several lives and then have a husband—at least the kind of marriage I had, which was incredibly intense. We were together all the time. And you can't live with someone on a twenty-four-hours-a-day basis, never be separated for years and years, and have the same freedom to grow and change and fly off to Hong Kong if you feel like it . . . it's irresponsible. That's why I say that somewhere along the line, one has to choose between the Life and the Project.

I think that for a lot of people who know both your name and who love your work, you have a special mystique. There are particularly a great number of women I know who admire you enormously.

But what you call mystique used to be called reputation.

I think in your case it's reputation and *mystique, because mystique in a way has to do with the fact that you're not a public celebrity who gossips in the media about whom you're going out with.*

Well, what serious writer ever did?

I could go through a list.

But those people have destroyed themselves as writers. I think it's death to one's work to do that. Surely, the body of the work of writers such as Hemingway or Truman Capote would be on a higher level if they hadn't been public figures. There *is* a choice between the work and the life. It's not only a choice between how much you manifest yourself in the ways that the media invite you to, but just how much you go out altogether.

There's a story of Jean Cocteau—to take an example of a writer I really admire—who, when he was in his late teens or early twenties, went to see Proust, who was already in his cork-lined room. Cocteau brought him some of his work, and Proust said, You really could be a great writer, but you have to be careful about society. Go out a little bit, but don't make it a main part of your life. And Proust spoke as someone who, in the early part of his life, had lived a very social, what we would call café-society or jet-set life in Paris, but he knew that there was a time when you had to choose between the work and the life. It's not just a question of whether you're going to give interviews or talk about yourself—it's a question of how much you live in society, in that vulgar sense of society—and of having a lot of silly times that seem glamorous to you and to other people.

But think of the Goncourt Brothers, who wouldn't have written what they did unless they frequented parties almost every night in Paris during the Second Empire. In a way, they were extraordinarily brilliant but high-class gossip types.

But they were also social historians using both the novel and documentary forms. Even Balzac did that. The problem, however, is a little different in the twentieth century since the opportunities are so much greater. I'm not saying that one has to be in a cork-lined room, but I think that one must have enormous discipline, and the vocation of the writer is, in some deep way, antisocial, just as it is for painters. Somebody once asked Picasso why he never traveled—he never took trips or went abroad. He went from Spain to Paris and then moved to the south of France, but he never went anywhere. And he said: I travel in my head. I do think there are those choices, and perhaps you don't feel them so much when you're young—and probably you shouldn't—but later on, if you want to go beyond something that is simply good or promising to the real fulfillment and risk-taking of a big body of work, then that only becomes a possibility for a writer or a painter after years of work, and you have to stay home.

In the mid-1970s, you, along with many other writers, were asked to draw a self-portrait that was later included in a book entitled Self-Portrait: Book People Picture Themselves. *And for yours, you simply drew a Jewish star, above which you wrote a saying by Confucius: "Each of us is meant to rescue the world." In a sense, one could half-jokingly say that you were actually adhering to the religious prohibition against drawing the human image.*

Yes, I was asked to draw myself, and I did it in thirty seconds—and that's, of course, the best way to do it, because if I had thought about it I would have been paralyzed. It's very funny, but I'm about to take drawing lessons with the artist Mary Frank. It's not that I now want to be an artist, I just want to learn how to draw in a nineteenth-century way—I want to draw the way John Ruskin drew the buildings in Venice. I want to be able to draw as a form of notation, of rendering.

What you noticed about my having drawn a nonfigurative self-portrait is true, but that's also because I didn't want to represent myself. I publish a book of stories called *I, etcetera*, and already all the complexity and dilemmas are there. In fact, a couple of the stories are autobiographical, but it's *I, etcetera*—and that's already to say that I'm putting the "I" in quotation marks. I don't think that I'm *expressing* myself. The point of my work is not to express *me*. I can *lend* myself to a work.

That reminds me of the statement by Montaigne that Godard quotes in his film Vivre sa vie: *"Lend yourself to others but give yourself to yourself."*

Yes, I can lend myself. But if something that actually happens to a character I'm writing about seems to fit perfectly, I might as well use it rather than to make up something entirely different. So I sometimes lend things from my own life because they seem to work, but I don't think that I'm representing *myself*. Let's assume Mary Frank has the patience, and I have the discipline, to actually learn to draw: I can't imagine that I would draw myself—I would *use* myself, among other things, as material. But what I'm interested in is the world. All my work is based on the idea that there really is a world, and I really feel as if I'm in it.

So you're in the world, and the world's in you.

Yes, I feel as if I'm paying attention to the world. I'm very aware of and fascinated by what is the *not* me, and I'm interested and drawn to understand it.

But what about the world that's in you?

It's true, obviously, but I don't find that metaphor very useful. I want to get away from solipsism, which is the great temptation of the modern sensibility—to think that it's all in your head.

Isn't your novel Death Kit *concerned with this idea?*

Yes, *Death Kit* is like getting lost inside one's head.

Don't you say in that book that living inside one's head is death?

Exactly. *Death Kit* and *Illness as Metaphor* are both about the same thing. The latter is based on reflections that I was led to make because I got sick, and I had to think about these things to try to save my life. But they're the reflections of somebody who was already on to those sorts of problems in the first place. What I came to feel was that these psychological theories of illness are not only culpabilizing but also a form of solipsism because you actually die if you don't get the proper medical help.

What fascinates me imaginatively may not at all be what draws me humanly, though I don't want to make that kind of separation because it sounds stupid. I assume responsibility for my writing because I know that it comes from me and that I'm the person who writes it. But I don't think my life is organized in the same way or around the same things as the writing is. I'm not writing autobiographically, I'm following my fantasies, and my fantasies are fantasies about the world, they're not about my doing those things. They are a fascination with the fact that these things exist, but I don't experience them as personal solicitations, as many people do. And I don't say that this is good, it's just another way of being. As I said, the things I write about are not necessarily those things that attract me. There are many things I write about that I not only have no personal experience of but I'm not even tempted to *have* any personal experience of.

Would it be fair to say that you feel as if you somehow transcend those things?

I don't know if it's transcendence. Transcendence is a positive word. I mean, if I would speak of it negatively, I might say it was *disassociation,* so I wouldn't speak about it either way. Giving free rein to my imagination is like a vehicle that takes me someplace else—it precisely takes me out of what I do and think and feel and how I live and what my relations with people are. And that's what I like about it, and why I don't like to write autobiographically. I want to write about things that I imagine or things that are happening out in the world, and *not* me.

But what is not *you might be just as much a part of you as thinking and feeling are.*

Sure. It's not that I'm *not* expressing myself, but that's not the model that I like. This is, as everyone has said, a period of self-consciousness. No serious writer today is naïve. You could have really serious writers in the past who were innocent in the sense of their relation to the problems of form and what they were doing. They were carried along by a certain kind of consensus, and if they were lucky enough to live in a high cultural moment when the materials that were offered to them were so wonderful . . . well, like Baroque music. You hardly hear any Baroque music that isn't good—although of course some Baroque compositions are better than others—because the form and language of music at that time were on such a high level, and we're not in a period like that anymore. Most writers I know—and I certainly include myself—now feel that every book has to be something different.

It seems to me that every story in I, etcetera *differs one from the other.*

There are eight stories in *I, etcetera,* and to me they are eight different ways of doing something. I think that today everything is a leap, a risk, a danger, and that's the excitement and intensity of it—to try to stretch and transcend oneself. And in order to have the kind of concentration that's necessary to do this, one does have to work, not in innocence, but in a state of intense *interiorness* that can be diffused or dissipated if you lend yourself too much to what people want you to do and be, or if you're in too much contact with what people think you're doing and with what they write about you.

Many people have a very nearsighted and conventional view of American fiction and poetry and tend to forget about the fascinating writings of, for example, Mina Loy, Link Gillespie, Harry Crosby, and especially Laura Riding and Paul Goodman. I've just finished reading Goodman's great novel The Empire City, *as well as his extraordinary* John-son *stories that he wrote in the early 1930s, when he was twenty-one years old.*

Absolutely. Well, you've mentioned two persons who have been models for me: Laura Riding's *Progress of Stories* really set a standard of writing. Almost nobody knows about this work and nobody's doing anything as good as that now—and not only are they not continuing it, they're not anywhere up to that. And, like you, I think that Paul Goodman's *Johnson* stories are one of the major accomplishments of twentieth-century American literature. [The eight original *Johnson* stories, which explore the relational intertwinings among three young New Yorkers—two men and one woman—are included in Goodman's *The Breakup of Our Camp: Stories, 1932–1935*, published in 1978 by Black Sparrow Press.] I think he could have been *the* great fiction writer of our time, but he also had these very fierce intellectual and political passions and got more and more involved with essay writing, so that the fiction became thinner and thinner. But those stories that he wrote when he was in his early twenties are one of the great triumphs of literature.

One of the things I do at four in the morning when I can't sleep is, instead of counting sheep, invent anthologies in my head, and one of my notions is to do a volume of short fiction by writers like Laura Riding and Paul Goodman. But I believe very much that all of this will be sorted out and that they will eventually find their audience. [In a journal entry dated August 20, 1978, in Sontag's *As Consciousness Is Harnessed to Flesh: Journals and Notebooks, 1964–1980*, she proposes "An Ideal Story Anthology" that includes works such as Robert Walser's "Kleist in Thun," Italo Calvino's "The Distance of the Moon," Laura Riding's "A Last Lesson in Geography," and Paul Goodman's "The Minutes Are Flying by Like a Snowstorm."]

I have to say, however, that from what I hear in the conversations I have with people today, there now seems to be a wholesale discrediting of what has been called modernism or the avant-garde. Everybody is so busy getting off that bus and saying that it's no good, that it's bankrupt, that it's beyond and behind us, that it's been proven to be shallow — even Roland Barthes has said this to me. The people I know who ten years ago were talking about Robbe-Grillet and Godard are now talking about Tolstoy and Colette. And I want very much to go against that general tendency. Not by using words like *modernism* and *avant-garde* — those words are tired and need to be retired. But if I want to think about how to write fiction, I'm going to read Laura Riding or the early stories of Paul Goodman, and I'm amazed by the extent to which modern work—the attempt to find new forms—is not even a project that is defended anymore.

When I started writing in the early sixties, I was defending the "modern," particularly in literature, because the prevailing approach was very philistine. And for about ten years, the views that I espoused became more and more common. But during the past five years, it's not as if people have gone back to the position they held before—it's worse. Before, they didn't like this stuff because they were ignorant, they didn't even know about it. Now they don't like it because they think they know something about it and feel superior to it. So you actually have to defend Schönberg or Joyce or Merce Cunningham.

There's a mean-spiritedness regarding high-modern art now that's so discouraging that I don't even feel like entering the fray in the essay form. I really had the feeling that by the end of the sixties the battle had been won, but it was a very transient victory. When I hear someone telling me that they don't like Dostoyevsky because he's so *chaotic,* I say, Wait a minute! You could say that the reason for this is that people have had enough, that they need to rest awhile. But I wonder, I wonder: Why should they be allowed to rest? [*laughing*]

At the climactic moment of your film Brother Carl, *the title character miraculously gets a mute girl to talk, and in your introduction to your screenplay for the film you write: "The only interesting action in life is a miracle or the failure to perform a miracle; and miracles are the only subject of profound interest left for art." Do you actually believe in miracles?*

I think that there are extraordinary things that happen and that can change everything, that an action can be the equivalent of the epiphany of consciousness, and that something can actually happen that doesn't seem warranted—though I don't mean that it can't be explained, because everything can be explained after the fact, even if only explained by chance—you know, a stopped clock is right twice a day.

Who said that?

I don't know, I think I read it in *Mad* magazine [*laughing*]. So if by miracle you mean something that can't be explained, that's almost a meaningless notion because, as I said, one can always discover antecedents that produce it. There's no event that happens that's not in some sequence of events, and therefore you can devise some kind of explanations for it. But still there are things that happen that don't seem to be warranted, or what you'd expect, and it's as if they open up a gap in which a more intense or creative or daring action can take place, and it's those seeming breaks in the continuities of things that are like epiphanies.

They're not always good, by the way, and sometimes they're awful. You can in part, for example, analyze Hitler this way. Everything he said and did has its precedents in German history, yet somebody like him who got it together and made it effective in the way that he did was really carrying it one step beyond anything else. And there's good reason to think that it would never have gone as far as it did without Hitler. It wasn't just a question of ideas or organization, it was a question of the demonic power this man had over other people.

I've experienced that in my own life and in the lives of others, and it fascinates me as a subject for fiction and art. As I said, I would connect it to the notion of something like an epiphany. It's also like a new beginning, but like every other idea it can be cheapened and debased beyond recognition. So in my film *Brother Carl*, it was important for me to show Carl *not* performing a miracle—not being able to resuscitate a woman who's just drowned—before he actually performs one.

There's a reason why traditional religious wisdom has been esoteric and often requires a kind of initiation to give evidence that you're prepared to receive it, because it's not for just everybody. You can say anything in any context—the nature of modern communication systems is that anything can be said, any context is equivalent to any other context so that things can be placed in many different contexts at the same time, like photography. But there's something profoundly compromising about that situation. Of course, there's also a great advantage to it because it allows for a liberty of action and consciousness that people have never had before. But it means that you can't keep original or profound meanings intact because inevitably they're dis-appointed, adulterated, transformed, and transmuted—it's a world in which everything is being recycled and recom-bined and things are being reduced to a common denomi-nator. So when you launch an idea for a fantasy or a theme or an image to the world, it has this tremendous career that you can't possibly control or limit. And that's perhaps an-other more immediate reason why one is tempted to be silent sometimes. You want to share things with other peo-ple, but on the other hand you don't want to just feed the machine that needs millions of fantasies and objects and products and opinions to be fed into it every day in order to keep on going.

Four months after we started this interview in Paris, I phoned you when you had returned to New York City to ask when we could complete our conversation, and you said, "We should do it soon because I may change too much." That surprised me.

Why? It seems so natural [*laughing*]. I feel I'm changing all the time, and that's something that's hard to explain to people, because a writer is generally thought to be someone who's either engaging in self-expression or else doing work to convince or change people along the lines of his or her views. And I don't feel that either of those models makes much sense for me. I mean, I write partly in *order* to change myself so that once I write about something I don't have to think about it anymore. And when I write, it actually *is* to get rid of those ideas. That may sound contemptuous of the public, because obviously when I've gotten rid of those ideas, I've passed them on as things that I believe — and I *do* believe them when I write them — but I don't believe them *after* I've written them because I've moved on to some other view of things, and it's become still more complicated . . . or perhaps more simple. So that makes it a little bit difficult to talk about the work because people may be interested in doing so, but having done it, I'm already someplace else.

In a way, it sounds like a firefly that at the very moment you see its light you realize that it's in fact already flown off somewhere else.

Yes, and that seems arrogant or irresponsible to people — sort of like hit-and-run — since I don't want to talk about it anymore. And on the other hand, I don't want to talk about the *new* thing either because I'm still working on it.

In your story "Debriefing," you talk about the desire to "change your feelings altogether, like getting your blood pumped out and replaced." And in "Old Complaints Revisited," the protagonist says: "You can't become other than what you are. Only more or less what you are. You can't walk over your own feet." Throughout I, etcetera, characters are trying to become someone else, someone "other."

Well, to become the "other" not in the sense of a *specific* other, but to change your life. And it's not the "other" in the sense of the "opposite," it may be just . . . well, like to wake up. I hate the feeling that I'm just executing what I already know or have already imagined. I like to *not* know where I'm going, and at the same time to be quite a way down the road. I don't like to be at the beginning, but I don't like to see the end, either.

Perhaps you prefer to be in the middle—like Dante in the middle of his journey.

Yes, I always feel I'm in the middle, but more toward the beginning than the end. I always have the impression that the work is apprentice work, and that if I can just finish it, then afterward I'll really do something good [*laughing*].

In your story "Project for a Trip to China," you refer to the cardinal directions—east, south, center, west, and north— and assign to them emotional equivalences such that east is anger, south is joy, west is grief, north is fear, and the center is sympathy. A center of sympathy seems to me such a beautiful and calming notion. So maybe we could talk about being in the center *as well as being in the* middle *of things.*

Sure, because what's so wonderful about language is that we have these positive and negative words for the same thing. That's why language is an infinite treasure. Think of the old joke that everybody knows: I'm firm, you're stubborn, and he's a pig-headed fool—three words of very different values to express the same behavior. So perhaps you can say that being in the middle is somewhat tainted as a description. I don't mean that it was for Dante, but when we say *in the middle*, we think of someone who wants to remain equidistant from certain alternatives because he or she is afraid to take sides. But being in the *center*—isn't that interesting? The whole thing changes.

To me, being in the center *suggests a sense of timelessness.*

Yes, one can think of it in the time sense. But "being in the center" is opposed to being marginal, and you don't want to be in the *margin* of your own consciousness, or your own experience, or your own time. John Calvin, of all people, said, "The world is sloped on either side, therefore place yourself in the middle of it." Meaning that you can fall off. We all know in our own lives that people are falling off the world all the time—they get onto that slope and then they start to slide. And that's *another* sense of being in the middle. But to be on level ground is what you want to do because life is very complicated and you don't want to just be hanging on by your bitten-down fingernails on one end of things, which is what happens to a lot of people because they can't see anymore. And from where they're hanging, it's just a struggle not to fall off completely.

It's said that J. S. Bach, when he was performing with a group of instrumentalists, preferred playing the alto or tenor parts because he could listen more intently to the more individualized soprano and bass lines. So by being in the middle, he could truly hear what was going on around him.

That's so interesting about Bach. I think it's wonderful. There's an active notion of neutrality that people don't understand. Transcendent neutrality isn't an attitude of "I won't take sides," it's compassion. Where you do see more than just what separates people or sides.

In the context of middles and ends, I wanted to ask you about your own "personal" beginnings. In "Project for a Trip to China," you talk of your own "desert childhood" that made you "an intractable lover" of heat and of the tropics.

I had a completely rootless childhood. In fact, I lived in many different places when I was a child. There was one place I lived in, however, that made the greatest impression on me, and that was southern Arizona. That's *imaginatively* my childhood. The rest of my so-called childhood was spent in Los Angeles, where I attended North Hollywood High School.

There are all these geographical oppositions that people set up, between California and New York, between northern and southern California, between New York and Paris.

But I like that. I like living in two places at once. That's the way I've tried to lead my life during the past ten years, ever since I've had the freedom to do so.

Susan Sontag

Are New York and Paris opposites to you in some way?

I live in Paris rather than some other place in Western Europe—although it could have been Rome—because I have friends there and because French is the only foreign language that I speak really properly. And I like to be in a place that's not the United States.

And you seem to have a special affinity with French life and culture.

Sure I do. I did. That's how I ended up there to begin with. I had an imaginary France in my head that consisted of Valéry and Flaubert and Baudelaire and Rimbaud and Gide. But it had nothing to do with the France that exists today at all, it was *that* France in my head that mattered a lot to me. I knew that that was the past, but I liked being on the site, in that beautiful architecture where these things had happened, and hearing that language.

Going from Tucson to Los Angeles was an enormous change. And then after finishing high school in L.A., I went to Berkeley, and then to the University of Chicago, and then to graduate school at Harvard. I spent a little time in California again, and then I came to New York. People think that I'm a New Yorker, but I only arrived here when I was twenty-six . . . and I came very much in the spirit of

Masha finally getting to Moscow. I'd always wanted to live in New York and I found that finally I was going to get to do it. I'm a New Yorker by choice.

Conversely, I'm a New Yorker by birth, but when I was about to graduate from Columbia College and apply to graduate school, someone gave me a copy of Henry Miller's Big Sur and the Oranges of Hieronymus Bosch, *which set me California Dreaming. And then, as happened to you with Bill Haley and the Comets, I had a road–to–San Francisco epiphany when I turned on the radio one day and heard the Beach Boys' "Fun Fun Fun" for the first time. And I really think that it was at that moment that I decided once and for all to forget the Ivy League—or any other league—and apply only to California graduate schools. California was for me what Paris was for you. I occasionally ran into you at Columbia College, and I distinctly remember one time mentioning to you that I was hoping to go to graduate school in California, and you said, How can you do that? And I have to say that you sounded like the typical parochial New Yorker knocking the Golden State!*

But I feel I have the right to knock California because I know it so well! I go back there at least twice a year and have close friends in the Bay Area. But I must admit that most of my friends there are easterners who have transplanted themselves. I know very few people who spent their childhoods in California.

Similarly, I know very few people in New York who were actually born here.

Yes, but I infinitely prefer the Northeast. I feel that too many things have just not migrated to California—the connection with Europe, with the past, with the book world, with the world of feelings and concerns and energies that are represented by nineteenth-century literature, to give it a very dumb name. It's too *remote* in California.

But that's what's so great about it. There actually is there there—but perhaps one could say that it is more like Gary Snyder than Robert Lowell—though, ironically, one of the most moving poetry readings I ever attended was one that Robert Lowell gave in Berkeley in 1965.

Well, I do feel the pull of both, too. It's the privilege of the writer to be "in the middle," as we talked about that before, and I want to honor and express those different kinds of longings. And since I'm not really a polemicist at all, I don't have to decide the way D. H. Lawrence decided what people ought to give up and what to hang on to. I don't know how to give up anything [*laughing*]. But in terms of this moral geography we're talking about, I, as I said, prefer New York . . . with, let's say, access to the Mediterranean or to California. You have to move around. I couldn't live twelve months or even ten months a year in New York. This is a totally artificial life. But so what? You have to create your own space—a space that has a lot of silence in it and a lot of books.

New York is the place I feel loyal to, I feel it's my base, and it's where I come back to. I've chosen it to be my central place because most of the people I'm close to are here—above all my son, my editors, and my close friends. And I have a niche in the cliff where I keep most of my books. But the one thing that is devastatingly absent in New York is nature of any kind. You're not in contact with anything that's normally living and dying. You can't lie on your back on the ground and look up at the sky at night and see a sky full of stars, which is something that teaches you a lot about your own mortality and your place in the universe—I mean, it's both terrifying and wonderful. In New York you just go from building to building.

So you don't have Kant's "starry sky above" but only the "moral law within."

[*Laughing*] Yes, I really miss the stars. But there's a blue sky half the year here, which is not true of Paris. And the light is wonderful. So there's something to connect it.

This discussion reminds me of the cliché that culture is a function of geography.

People define themselves to an amazing degree by their ideas of place. I met a woman recently in Indiana—a very interesting, intelligent woman who's lived there for many years—and she finally decided, now that her kids have grown up, to move east. And she said: "Well, I think the right city for me would be Boston. It's *east*, and it's got a lot of *things*, it's close to Europe, and New York would be too much." But this is totally on the level of myth. She defines herself as a woman who can make the move from Indiana to Boston, but not from Indiana to Manhattan because that's a much *bigger* move. In fact, it's not.

But I know what she means.

I do understand what she means, too, but it's still based on a myth that's so alive. She still has to sell her house in Indiana, get herself a job in the Boston area, set up a whole new life, which is just as much trouble to do in the Boston area as the New York area, but she's decided on the basis of a cultural fantasy that Boston is quieter, a little less hectic, not so much stimulation.

But that's true too!

Right. But it's on the basis of that myth that Boston is Boston and New York is New York. Whereas somebody else might say, Well, boy, I've spent twenty years in Indiana and now I want the real thing. What they're doing is defining themselves. It's not as if she said, Well, maybe I'll go to Boston for five years and then I might feel ready for New York. But you know that if you live in a city then all kinds of people live in it in any case.

But you yourself, feeling drawn to California and New York, still prefer one over the other and are therefore, in a way, also involved with that myth.

Yes, but I'm involved in it perhaps to a second degree, in the sense that when I say that I like to live in New York, I also mean that I like to live in a place where people have chosen to be. The first thing one says about New York *is* on the level of myth. It's a world capital and the cultural capital of the country. For better or worse, it is. There are more people here doing things than in any other single place. So if you live in this place, it's like saying, Okay, I want to live in a place where *more* things are happening than I can possibly have time for. It's not that I'm going to do all of them, but I want to know that I *could* do them, and I want to have that choice. And another reason for being here is that I want to run into people who are ambitious and restless. You meet a Californian and they say, Hi! . . . and then there's a big silence [*laughing*]. That's okay. But I get restless.

The best thing is to get restless in California and say Hi! in New York.

Exactly. And I have to tell you that when I first came to New York, I did feel that New Yorkers were short, rude, and mean—although I think that it's a little better now. I was very used to western friendliness and hospitality and kindness, and people there were kinder, more polite, and less abrasive. The way I talk, moreover, and the way I smile a lot is very Californian. The way I'm not defensive or guarded or suspicious of people.

Yet in "Project for a Trip to China," you wrote: "Somewhere, someplace inside myself, I am detached."

But I don't identify completely with the voices in my stories. I don't think I've ever been detached. And insofar as a character speaking in the first person in one of my stories says that, that's not me. I do think that I have been hiding out at different times in my life the way artists tend to do, hiding out with my work and with reading, hiding out with a couple of friends, fearful of the world because people were going to tell me to stop doing what I was doing, and I didn't even want to hear or be bothered by those cues. Many people, particularly women, have asked me, "How come you didn't get discouraged? You must have been given to understand that you shouldn't have the ambitions that you had." I feel I never was discouraged because I never listened to that message, but in order not to hear it, I certainly must have had my hearing apparatus turned off in some way. So if detached, detached only in the sense that I instinctively protected myself against things that could have discouraged me. Like people saying, "You don't want to do that, or you'll never get a husband!" [*laughing*]

In your film Duet for Cannibals, *there's a scene showing someone bandaging another person's head, which seemed at that moment to convey the idea of the connection between the idea of identity and the wound. And in your story "Unguided Tour," you wrote: "How far from the beginning are we? When did we first start to feel the wound? . . . This staunchless wound,*

Susan Sontag

the great longing for another place. To make this place an-other." Don't you think that this suggests, in microcosm, a lot of what we've been talking about throughout our interview?

And that's why that story is the end of I, *etcetera.*

But I wanted to connect it to the beginning of that book. In that first story, "Project for a Trip to China," you write: "To be good one must be simpler. Simpler, as in a return to origins." The Austrian critic Karl Kraus once remarked: "Origin is our goal." Is it yours?

I don't want to return to my origins. I think my origins are just a starting point. My sense of things is that I've come very far. And it's the distance I have traveled from my origins that pleases me. That's because I have, as I mentioned to you, this rootless childhood and an extremely fragmented family. I have in New York many close relatives whom I've never seen. I don't know who they are. And that just has to do with my being a member of a family that collapsed or disinte-grated or that has been dispersed. I don't have anything to go back to, and I can't imagine what it would be that I would find. I've spent my whole life getting away. But, of course, many people do have something, and that's wonderful.

I think of myself as self-created—that's my working il-lusion. I even think of myself as an autodidact despite the fact that I had a very good education—Berkeley, Chicago, Harvard. But I still think that, basically, I'm self-taught. I never was anybody's disciple or protégée, I wasn't launched by someone, it wasn't because I was somebody's lover or wife or daughter that I "made my career." I never expected it to be otherwise. But of course I don't think it's awful to accept help either. If you can get help, fine. But I like the fact that I did it myself. I thought I would have to, I accepted it as a challenge. And it excited me to do it that way.

You know, I have a persistent fantasy—of course I'll never do it because I don't know how to do it, and perhaps I also don't have enough time left to live to make it worthwhile—but I do have this fantasy of tearing everything up and of starting all over again under a pseudonym which no one would know was Susan Sontag. I would love to do that, it would be wonderful to start again and not have the burden of the work that's already done. I think I would probably do things a little differently . . . and maybe not. Maybe I'm kidding myself. Maybe if I'd publish something under the name of . . . whatever, everyone would roar with laughter and say, "That's obviously Susan Sontag!" because I can't write in any way that would not be easily recognizable. But I just want to say that my notion is very much that of going further and further, of new beginnings, and of *not* going back to origins.

Ultimately, I think that we must destroy false and demagogic interpretations . . . and I do identify with that enterprise. In more grandiose moments, I think of myself as being involved in this task of lopping off heads—as Hercules did with the Hydra—knowing perfectly well, of course, that this same kind of false consciousness and demagogical thinking will turn up someplace else. But I will go on doing this as long as I can, and then I know that other people will continue to do it, too.

I said earlier that the task of the writer is to pay attention to the world, but obviously I think that the task of the writer, as I conceive of it for myself, is also to be in an aggressive and adversarial relationship to falsehoods of all kinds . . . and, once again, knowing perfectly well that this is an endless task, since you're never going to end falsehood or false consciousness or systems of interpretation. But there should always be some people in any generation who are attacking these things, and that's what disturbs me so much about most places in the world where the only criticism of society comes from the state itself. I think there should always be freelance people who, however quixotic it may be, are trying to lop off a couple of more heads, trying to destroy hallucination and falsehood and demagogy— and making things more complicated, because there's an inevitable drift towards making things more simple. But for me, the most awful thing would be to feel that I'd agree with the things I've already said and written—*that* is what would make me most uncomfortable because that would mean that I had stopped thinking.

Acknowledgments

■

I am particularly grateful to Susan Sontag's son, the writer David Rieff, and to my editor Steve Wasserman, who was one of her most devoted friends. Without their encouragement and guidance, this book would not have been possible. Special thanks to Jann Wenner, who originally commissioned my interview with Susan Sontag for *Rolling Stone*. A shortened version appeared in the October 4, 1979, issue of the magazine; it is being printed here in its entirety for the first time.

I am also greatly indebted to John Donatich, the director of Yale University Press; to its editorial director, Christopher Rogers; and to my manuscript editor, Dan Heaton.

Index

Index

George, Saint, 24
Gide, André, 90
Gillespie, Link, 117
Godard, Jean-Luc, 55, 112
Golden Bowl, The (James), 88
Goncourt, Edmond de, 15, 110–11
Goncourt, Jules de, 15, 110–11
Goodman, Paul, 33, 104, 117–18
Gould, Glenn, xviii
Great Dictator, The (film), 96

Haley, Bill, 35–36
Hardwick, Elizabeth, 84, 87
Haydn, Franz Joseph, 82
Hellman, Lillian, xviii
Hemingway, Ernest, 110
Hercules, 22–24, 138
Hitler, Adolf, 121
Hobbes, Thomas, 70
Hopkins, Gerard Manley, 86
Hydra, 22, 24, 138

I, etcetera (Sontag), xvi, 50, 63, 98, 112, 116, 136
Iliad (Homer), 91
illness: and compassion, 14–15; in literature, 91, 92; as metaphor, 21–22, 24, 25–28, 63, 91; psychological theories of, 17–18;

and spiritual values, 15–17; victim's responsibility for, 19–20. *See also* cancer; syphilis; tuberculosis
Illness as Metaphor (Sontag), xvi, 1–2, 4, 5–6, 15, 17, 25, 28, 91, 98, 114; cover of, 22–24, 45
Inauguration of the Pleasure Dome (film), xv
In the Realm of the Senses (film), 43

James, Henry, xi, xviii, 88–89
Joan of Arc, 68, 69
Joyce, James, 61, 67, 69, 90

Kafka, Franz, 13, 60, 64, 85, 87, 90
Kant, Immanuel, 131
Kinks, the, 73
Konrád, György, 64
Kraus, Karl, 136

Laing, R. D., 28, 37
Lawrence, D. H., 130–31
"Letter to Borges, A" (Sontag), xx
leukemia, 27–28
Lipatti, Dinu, 27
London, Jack, 89
Lowell, Robert, 130

· 142 ·

About the Author

Jonathan Cott is the author of numerous books, including *Days That I'll Remember: Spending Time with John Lennon and Yoko Ono, Dinner with Lenny: The Last Long Interview with Leonard Bernstein, Conversations with Glenn Gould,* and *Back to a Shadow in the Night: Music Writings and Interviews, 1968–1971.* A contributing editor for *Rolling Stone* magazine since its inception, he has also written for the *New York Times* and the *New Yorker.* He lives in New York City.